S0-BZB-847

Teaching Your
Occupation
to Others

Teaching Your Occupation to Others

A Guide to Surviving the First Year

Second Edition

Paul A. Bott
California State University, Long Beach

Allyn and Bacon
Boston   London   Toronto   Sydney   Tokyo   Singapore

Executive Editor: Virginia Lanigan
Editorial Assistant: Kris Lamarre
Editorial-Production Administrator: Joe Sweeney
Editorial-Production Service: Walsh & Associates, Inc.
Composition Buyer: Linda Cox
Manufacturing Buyer: Suzanne Lareau
Cover Administrator: Suzanne Harbison

Copyright © 1998, 1987 by Allyn & Bacon
A Viacom Company
160 Gould Street
Needham Heights, MA 02194

Internet: www.abacon.com
America Online: keyword: College Online

All rights reserved. No part of this material protected by this copyright notice may be reproduced or utilized in any form or by any means, electronic or mechanical, including photocopying, recording, or by any information storage and retrieval system, without written permission from the copyright owner.

Library of Congress Cataloging-in-Publication Data

Bott, Paul A.
    Teaching your occupation to others : a guide to surviving the
first year / Paul A. Bott. — 2nd ed.
      p.   cm.
    Includes bibliographical references and index.
    ISBN 0–205–27101–4
    1. Vocational teachers.   2. Occupational training.   3. Teaching.
I. Title.
LB1736.B68   1997
371.102—dc21   97–1295
                                                CIP

Printed in the United States of America
10 9 8 7 6 5 4 3 2   00 99

Contents

3. How People Learn   37
Some Principles of Learning

Preface

Because occupational education teachers are often hired right out of industry to begin teaching immediately, there is need of assistance in surviving the first year in the classroom. This book contains practical examples of methods and techniques needed by teachers to deal with the bureaucracy, the curriculum, and the students, from the first day of class through their first final examination. Students comment that the book is written in a language and style that is comfortable to new teachers and that it was written with their needs in mind.

This is the second edition of a book that was developed and used over a number of years in occupational teacher education courses at California State University, Long Beach. Since 1981, over 6000 beginning teachers in the CSULB program and countless others in teacher education programs around the country have used all or portions of this book to obtain part of their teacher education. My colleagues and their students at other institutions have offered many suggestions for improvement, most of which I have tried to incorporate in this edition. I am deeply indebted to all the teacher educators, teachers, and students who have offered comments and constructive criticism and advice for this edition. I would also like to thank those who reviewed this book: Ronald Galliher, University of Massachusetts, Boston; William E. Blank, University of South Florida; John D. Lynch, University of Massachusetts, Boston. I am especially indebted to my family for providing me with the time to spend writing instead of doing the laundry. It is to them and my many students that I dedicate this book.

1 Are You Sure You Really Want To Teach?

Paths to Becoming a Teacher

PEOPLE BECOME TEACHERS of occupational subjects for many different reasons and by a variety of routes. An overview of why people become teachers and descriptions of some of the ways to do so is presented in this chapter, followed by a discussion of several major reasons people have for choosing to teach. The second section contains a description of typical education and work experience requirements. Common licensure requirements are described in the third section, followed by the paths to becoming certified and for locating prospective employers. The last section contains some hints on how to succeed in your search for a teaching job.

Why People Become Teachers

Until recently, the public has viewed teaching as one of the noble professions. If you were to ask the teachers of fifty years ago, they would probably agree that theirs was a respected profession. Declining test scores, excessive student absenteeism, an increasing violence rate, and a host of other problems are drastically changing the picture of what a teacher is and why one chooses teaching in the first place.

Second Career

Most people are achievement and goal oriented. They respond well to challenges and are proud of what they do for a living. Their jobs become a major part of their reason for existing. But, sooner or later, for many people the challenge is gone . . . jobs become routine. Most of us become so adept at our work that often we do not even think about it while we are doing it. We are good at what we do, but that old spark just isn't there anymore. Most of us who teach believe that since we know so much about our occupation, we can teach it to others. Teaching is a rewarding career, and the switch from doing to teaching often renews that spark, creating a new challenge, and still does not take us away from our first love . . . working at our occupation. In essence then, teaching becomes a second career, not after, but in addition to, what we already do.

People Oriented

When asked, most people will respond to the why-do-you-want-to-be-a-teacher question with "I like kids." By the time most people become teachers of occupational subjects, "kids" are anyone under twenty-five. Most students in occupational programs are between 16 and 24, but each year as the economy shifts and jobs change, more and more adults return to school to learn a new occupation or to upgrade their current skills. "I like kids" is not enough. We need to like people . . . all kinds of people. You will see later (in Chapters 3 and 4) that all of the different people we teach learn and work differently. Teachers must accept all students for who they are and what they wish to become.

Injury

Injuries or debilitating diseases that incapacitate workers cause a disproportionate number of people to leave productive employment each year. Many of them possess an extraordinary amount of knowledge about their jobs that, if given the opportunity, they could share with others. Although teaching is definitely not a sedentary occupation, people with disabilities (even ones that would keep them from actually performing a job) can and do make excellent teachers. Today, nearly all classrooms are accessible to students with disabilities and therefore to teachers with disabilities. What is important is the occupational experience and the desire to share it that make a good teacher.

Working Environment

Teaching an occupation, especially in the so-called heavy trades, is generally much cleaner and less physically demanding than actually performing the work. In addition, teachers usually teach all aspects of a job, while workers may perform the same aspect over and over each day. For this reason and because all the students are different, teaching is a diverse occupation.

Since teaching an occupation generally is a second career (remember, we are all teachers of an occupation), it is essential that we not only learn all there is to know about teaching, but we also have to stay abreast of all changes and developments in our other career—the occupation we are teaching. Teaching an occupation, therefore, affords us the opportunity for much intellectual stimulation and growth.

A number of creature comforts come with the territory. Most schools are in session about 180 days per year, leaving nearly three months of nonteaching time for the pursuit of other activities. Since pay stops when school is not in session, this "vacation" is sometimes just a vacation from the paycheck, but for many teachers of occupations, summer and other vacation times are ideal for renewing their occupational skills. Many school districts award salary points to occupational teachers for a specific number of hours "back on the job." All parties benefit from this—the teachers keep their skills and knowledge up-to-date, and the students benefit from the latest information. (The extra check never hurts either.)

Other fringe benefits include breaks at all national holidays and winter and spring recesses. Teachers usually work only six to seven hours per day in the classroom, but time must be allotted for preparation, grading papers, and extracurricular school activities, so the day often extends to 9 or 10 hours and may include weekend duty.

It's a Profession

As discussed, teachers were once highly regarded. Although their reputation has somewhat diminished, for the most part this is still true. Teaching is a profession with a specific (if somewhat diverse) body of knowledge: pedagogy. It also has a unique vocabulary and more acronyms than any one person could ever master. Teaching has a code of ethics, and society still believes that what teachers do is important enough to warrant licensure. A code of ethics from one state may be found in the Appendix. The code of ethics is an attempt to provide educators with some guidelines regarding the expected way of speaking and behaving as a teacher. Teachers of occupational subjects are also expected to dress like a professional. This often requires purchasing a new wardrobe, because the clothing worn to perform an occupation might not necessarily be the same as that worn to teach the occupation.

Not just anyone can become a teacher, especially a teacher of occupational subjects. Just as attorneys, physicians, psychologists, and nurses periodically have to demonstrate their competence through re-licensure and by completing continuing education requirements, so do teachers. An educated people, some argue, is our most valuable natural resource. Teachers and schools are entrusted with the care and nurturing of that resource.

Paths to Becoming a Teacher

A guiding principle of occupational education is that a teacher of an occupation, in order to be effective and to realistically present what occurs on a job, has to have some actual work experience. A second principle is that occupational experience alone is not enough to make a teacher. We all know people who have a great deal of formal education, but who have never worked outside of the university. They may know all about an occupation, but they have never experienced the elation, frustration, or confusion of actually being a nurse or machinist or computer operator. These people can teach an idealized version of an occupation, but something will be missing. On the other hand, we all know people who know all there is to know about an occupation, but who have never developed the skills needed to communicate that knowledge to others. They, too, can teach in the classroom, but their *teaching* will probably frustrate all concerned.

For a variety of reasons, teachers of occupational subjects need work experience as well as formal education (both in their occupational subject and in methods of teaching). Some combinations of education and work experience that qualify people to teach occupational subjects are discussed in the following paragraphs.

Four-Year Degree Programs

Quite often, a bachelor's degree in a subject such as agriculture, nursing, industrial technology, or family and consumer sciences will serve as the primary preparation for teaching these occupations. But if we keep the two "principles" in mind, we realize that some actual work experience as a nurse, estimator, or dietician is necessary so that the subject is presented as it is practiced. Imagine someone who has a bachelor's degree in music with an emphasis in playing the piano. That person might be able to teach the basics of piano playing, but it is doubtful that he or she could teach someone the way to make a living playing the piano because the practical experience is missing. There is no set rule as to how much experience is "enough," but for teaching, a broad base is as important as a thorough, but narrow, base.

Three-Year Degree Programs

Many occupations, especially those in the health care fields, now have three-year in-school programs. These programs, like the four-year programs, provide a good theoretical and practical basis for performing an occupation. But no school, no matter how innovative, can accurately simulate the work-a-day world where so many practical skills are developed. State licensure laws for teaching usually require about twice as much work for three-year program graduates as for the bachelor's degree candidate. For example, if a state requires two years of work experience for baccalaureate degree holders, they will generally require three to four years for graduates of three-year programs.

Two-Year Degree Programs

In some states, nearly two-thirds of community college students graduate with an associate degree in an occupational field. These graduates not only have obtained basic skill and proficiency in an occupational subject, but they also have received a "general" education in subjects such as history, mathematics, science, art, and communication skills. Community college graduates in occupational subjects are well on the way to becoming skilled in an occupation, and, with practice, they will develop the basis for skills (such as communication) through their general education. Some two-year programs, such as nursing programs operated by hospitals, do not have general education as a component.

Remember the two principles: Occupational teachers need education about their subject, and they need experience in performing the jobs. Neither alone will suffice.

Certificate Programs

Many community colleges and regional or area vocational schools have intense one-year programs that are designed to get graduates into the job market with saleable skills. Graduates of certificate and two-year occupational programs generally will need from three to five years of full-time work experience in order to qualify for credentials to teach that occupation. A guideline is that the less formal education in a subject, the more work experience required.

Apprentice Preparation

Labor unions and employers provide many excellent apprenticeship programs. These programs combine on-the-job experience with classroom preparation for the skills, knowledge, and attitudes necessary to achieve success on the job. Apprentices work under the direction of skilled workers (journeypersons) and are taught many, if not most, skills under actual working conditions. In most states, time spent as an apprentice counts toward work experience requirements for teacher certification. Incidentally, teachers of the in-class portion of apprenticeship classes usually are state-certified teachers, and the classes are often given for credit in community colleges or vocational schools.

Informal Education

The largest group of occupational teachers is probably the group that is drawn directly from an occupation. They often have no formal education in the subject. This is not to say that they aren't educated . . . they just didn't get their education in a classroom, but rather have been educated by experience. They know virtually everything about an occupation because they have done it all. To qualify for initial certification, though, such individuals must have from five to ten years of on-the-job experience. They then are admitted to teacher preparation programs to develop the teaching skills.

What to Do to Become a Teacher

Requirements for teaching different subjects vary among states and localities. A broad overview of licensing requirements and some ideas as to where to start looking for a teaching job are presented in this section.

Credential Requirements

Teaching credential (or licensing) requirements vary from state to state and within states by educational level. For example, a state may require adherence to one set of criteria for teaching in secondary schools or regional occupational programs, and adherence to an entirely different set of criteria for teaching in a community college or other postsecondary school. It is likely, however, that the requirements will be similar.

Many states have provisions for teachers of occupational subjects allowing issuance of a temporary certificate if certain minimum criteria are met. These criteria almost always include adequate work experience (see preceding sections in this chapter), demonstrated competence in the occupation to be taught, and agreement to commence teacher education courses or activities within a specified time.

Some states require teachers to pass a state basic skills competency examination before they will issue a temporary certificate. Most states require prospective teachers to be fingerprinted and to undergo a thorough background check. A felony conviction will almost certainly preclude obtaining state certification.

Some school districts and community colleges have personnel who are specially trained to advise you of credential requirements. The courses and activities needed to complete credential requirements usually are offered only by colleges and universities. In many states, only specific universities and university programs are authorized to offer teaching credential courses.

Teaching credentials are your license to practice. State education codes prohibit paying a teacher who has practiced without credentials or with expired credentials, so maintaining a license is not only a legal responsibility but one that can drastically affect the pocketbook. This may not be true in private postsecondary schools. The department of education will provide a copy of the requirements for maintaining your credentials. In addition, contact a local university that is authorized to offer teacher education courses and enroll in those appropriate to your credential type. It is important for your professional effectiveness (and some would say your sanity) to get your teacher education underway as soon as possible. Teacher education courses will help you design and carry out effective instruction. In addition, you will find that your classmates have the same problems and frustrations as you do. Chatting at class breaks may lead to insights about your new profession.

Prospective Employers

University teacher education courses serve another important function—a source of teaching position announcements. Your classmates will usually teach in different schools and districts and will know of many position openings even before they are announced. They will be able to tell you whom to contact and, in many cases, give you tips on what to say.

Most universities with teacher education programs also operate placement offices for their students. They receive announcements from a wide geographic area about positions in many disciplines. Placement offices often help prepare your resumé and other forms and some duplicate them on request. Teaching positions are now routinely posted on the Internet.

Individual departments within the university (such as Agriculture, Nursing, Industrial or Technology Education, and Family and Consumer Sciences) also receive and post job announcements. Your professors often will advise you about the jobs being offered. Many professors are willing to write letters of reference.

Local, county, and state education offices may have a job "hotline" of sorts. Position openings are recorded and played back when a telephone number is dialed. Find out if the schools and districts in your area have such a service. Many schools and districts are now posting job announcements on electronic media such as the Internet.

Schools are turning increasingly to the media to advertise positions. Professional journals and newspapers (such as *Techniques,* the journal of the American Vocational Association, Phi Delta *Kappan,* and *Teacher*) have classified sections specifically devoted to teaching positions that are available. Some schools advertise in general circulation newspapers when seeking teachers.

Many school districts and some private schools announce job openings at professional conferences or conventions, such as the annual conference of the

American Vocational Association or the regional conferences of state vocational associations. In many cases, interviews are conducted at the conventions.

Public schools are not the only places that offer occupational preparation programs. The U.S. Armed Services offer the largest comprehensive occupational preparation programs in the country. Many of the teachers are civilians. Your local federal building will have an office that can advise you of the openings and locations.

Virtually every large city has private proprietary occupational schools. Some subjects typically taught at these schools include secretarial skills, cosmetology, computer occupations, nursing, medical assisting, and many of the skilled trades. Most proprietary schools announce position openings in the want ads of general circulation publications under the occupation to be taught.

Technological changes and other factors have brought about an increase in the number of "in-house" training programs in business and industry. Most large companies (over 250 employees) have a person who is responsible for training in the company. The larger companies retain full-time instructors for some subjects. Although many of these positions are filled from within the company, some instructors are hired from the outside. Position announcements are placed in trade or professional journals and general circulation publications.

One other source of jobs for teachers of occupational subjects is the employment and training or human resources development programs that are sponsored by government agencies. The most recent of these programs sponsored by the Federal government is the Job Training Partnership Act (JTPA). Teaching positions in these programs are normally announced by the local agency conducting the program, such as city and county governments. Some positions are announced in general circulation publications.

In all cases, the keys to finding the jobs are networking and looking. As in any other occupation, it is rare that a teaching position is offered out of the blue.

Getting a Teaching Job

As technology and the employment market fluctuate, new courses and programs are developed, and teaching positions in occupational subjects become available. This section contains information about position announcements and what to emphasize in applications and interviews.

Position Announcements

Announcements for positions teaching occupational subjects usually state the minimum qualifications for the job in terms of years of work experience, educational qualifications, and the type of credentials that applicants must possess or be eligible to obtain. Most announcements contain the salary range and the term (in months) of employment. Many position announcements contain a statement of ancillary duties such as curriculum development, student placement, and employer liaison.

Highly skilled people in business are often sought and actively recruited by other businesses. This just doesn't happen in education. People wanting a teaching position have to look for it themselves. This involves visiting placement offices as well as reading want ads in general circulation and professional publications.

When responding to a job announcement, write a cover letter to accompany your resume. In the letter, respond to specific items in the job announcement that you feel you are exceptionally qualified to do. Summarize your work experience and detail your activities with youth and adult groups (this will show your interest in and ability to work with diverse groups). Above all, be neat and precise. The people who hire teachers are looking for someone who can communicate clearly and effectively. Messy letters, misspelled words, incomplete sentences, and grammatical errors will get your application moved to the bottom of the stack. Have someone carefully proofread your resume and cover letter. Samples of a cover letter and resume may be found in the appendix.

The Interview

Although there are many books and articles on job interview techniques, a few comments are in order. Be prepared to discuss your occupational background and your ability to communicate. Before the interview, carefully think through your beliefs regarding the purposes of education and what qualities you feel make a good employee in your occupation; you can almost count on being asked such questions. It is doubtful that an interviewer for a teaching position would be enthusiastic about hiring someone whose thoughts are not coherent and who does not communicate well in a one-on-one situation.

Some things you will want to know about the position include the source of funding (is it a special project or a regular position?), the number and type of classes to be taught, and the type and quality of the facilities and equipment available. Being prepared to ask pertinent questions is just as important as your ability to answer the interviewer's questions. Sometimes the person or team conducting the interview either doesn't know or doesn't tell all there is to know about the position. In other words, some programs are not what they seem.

There Must Be a Catch Here Somewhere

It wouldn't be fair to conclude this chapter without sharing the downside of teaching. As with any other job in any other organization, there are politics in education. Saying the wrong thing or being perceived as being aligned with one group or individual can add difficulty to your teaching life. Schools and school systems are bureaucracies that take time to understand. Sometimes the most simple and common sense request can take months to resolve. You might remember the advertising slogan "This is not your father's Oldsmobile," meaning today's automobile is not the same as your father's. It is the same in teaching—today's students often do not resemble those you went to school with. Today proportionately more students arrive at the schoolhouse door with significantly more problems than at any time in history. Like scenes that we used to find only in futuristic movies, it is now routine to see security personnel and administrators roaming the halls of schools with walkie-talkies on the lookout for trouble and individuals who should not be in the schools. Students in some schools pass through metal detectors to discourage and intercept guns and knives at the front door. Other schools require students to wear identification cards that are scanned on entering the grounds.

Teachers are often expected to be substitute parents, birth control counselors, nutritionists, and conflict resolvers in addition to being a subject matter expert. Teaching is definitely not an occupation for someone looking for a slower pace of life!

Getting Ready

Many teachers of occupational subjects have only a few days to prepare before beginning to teach. If possible, obtain a course outline and attempt to gain access to your classroom facilities ahead of time. Try to prepare several days' lessons and activities before you meet your first students (see Chapter 5 for some hints on how to do this). Learn where tools, equipment, and supplies are stored. Get a "feel" for your facilities, you will be spending a lot of time in them.

Most of all—rest for a day or two before beginning work. Your first few weeks will be very hectic.

For Further Reading

Camp, W.G., and Heath-Camp, B. (1991). "On Becoming a Teacher: They Just Gave A Key and Said 'Good Luck.'" Berkeley, CA: National Center for Research in Vocational Education.

Fried, R. L. (1995). *The Passionate Teacher: A Practical Guide.* Boston: Beacon Press.

Scott, C.P. (1985). "That Critical First Year." *Vocational Education Journal* 60(6) 32–34.

Stine, M.B. (1986). "Preservice and Inservice Needs." *Vocational Education Journal* 61(2) 37–38.

2 Surviving the First Few Days

FORTUNATELY FOR TEACHERS and other school personnel, school usually doesn't start until the staff has had a day to get ready. Most of the time, the entire staff will assemble one or two days prior to the students' arrival for general and departmental faculty meetings and to open the classrooms and ready laboratories. Some of the things to be aware of during that first faculty meeting and the first few days of your career as a teacher are examined in this chapter.

The first and second sections contain some ideas and items to consider during the first day of meetings and getting acquainted and a list of things that need to be done just prior to or on the first day of instruction. The third and fourth sections contain hints to assist you in becoming comfortable with and growing in your new profession.

Initial School Contact

Someone has told you that if you can survive the first few days of teaching you can make it through anything, so you arrive at the school an hour earlier than the first scheduled meeting hoping to get a jump on the many activities. Your initial contact usually is with the school secretary who will inform you of sign-in and sign-out procedures. Most schools and districts, especially those with collective bargaining agreements, have definite hours during which teachers must be on campus. Learn what those hours are.

The school secretary also will tell you your room and laboratory assignment and will issue a form that enables you to get the keys you need to rooms and cabinets. While you are in the main office, you will probably be shown the locations of your mailbox and the teachers' workroom.

With your head buzzing with the expectations of a new job and a new career, you leave the main office and head for the custodian's office. "Why the custodian?" you ask. Because the head custodian is usually the keeper of the keys, and without them you will find it difficult getting into your room. The custodial staff has many responsibilities in addition to maintenance. They often act as the shipping and receiving department; they arrange for equipment repair and maintenance; and, in some schools, they assign parking spaces. You will have occasion to use all services performed by the custodial staff, so be sure to introduce yourself and tell them what your assignment will be.

Now that you have your keys, drop by your room and make sure that you have keys to everything in it. In the remaining few minutes before the general faculty meeting get to know your room and its contents . . . you will be spending a lot of time there over the next few months.

The First Faculty Meeting

It's nearly 9 o'clock, so you head for the room in which the first faculty meeting of the semester is about to start. You probably know only two people at that meeting, the principal (or dean) and your department head. If the faculty is large, locate one of them and find out where your department will sit. Quite often you will have a department meeting right after the school's general meeting.

Most faculty meetings include introductions of new faculty, overviews of the budget problems, descriptions of curricular additions, instructions on how to fill out this year's new forms, news from around the school and district, and, finally, a pep talk by the school administrator. Quite often in larger districts, the superintendent will address the faculty using videotape or closed circuit television. Pay close attention to the way people relate to one another in the general faculty meeting. During this one or two hour meeting you will often get a good idea of the political and administrative tenor in the school. Remember who does the talking, how they say it, and how well it is received by different members of the group. Take time to listen to others and observe your surroundings before forming opinions or making judgements about the administration and fellow faculty.

Unless there are a large number of new faculty, several items will not be covered in a general faculty meeting that you definitely need to know about. One of these is the "faculty handbook." Most school districts and educational institutions have some form of handbook that provides details of how the school is operated, school and district policies, state and local laws pertaining to school operation and teacher conduct, what to do in the event of emergencies, and dozens of other essentials. Get a copy of the faculty handbook as soon as you can and master the contents.

Another essential bit of information is the student handbook. Learn the school policies regarding what constitutes an offense and what the consequences of these behaviors are.

School Organization

Most educational organizations are administratively organized in similar fashions. Typically, one person is the education equivalent of the CEO. They are usually called "principal" in secondary schools and "president" in post-secondary institutions such as community colleges. There will usually be one or more vice-principals or vice-presidents, depending on the size of the school; several department heads; numerous supportive staff; and the faculty. Figure 2.1 contains two different school organizational structures with descriptive titles. Flow of information and direction will usually follow the paths from one position to the next.

Paperwork

At the department meeting, be sure to inquire about the paperwork that is required. You will discover that there are forms for everything and that each one has to be submitted by a specified hour or date. Some examples of forms include grade books, interim grade reports, attendance records, accident forms, hall passes, student communications, disciplinary reports, supply orders, and requests for equipment maintenance. Without a proper knowledge of forms and their whos and wheres, you will find it difficult to get everything done. Most

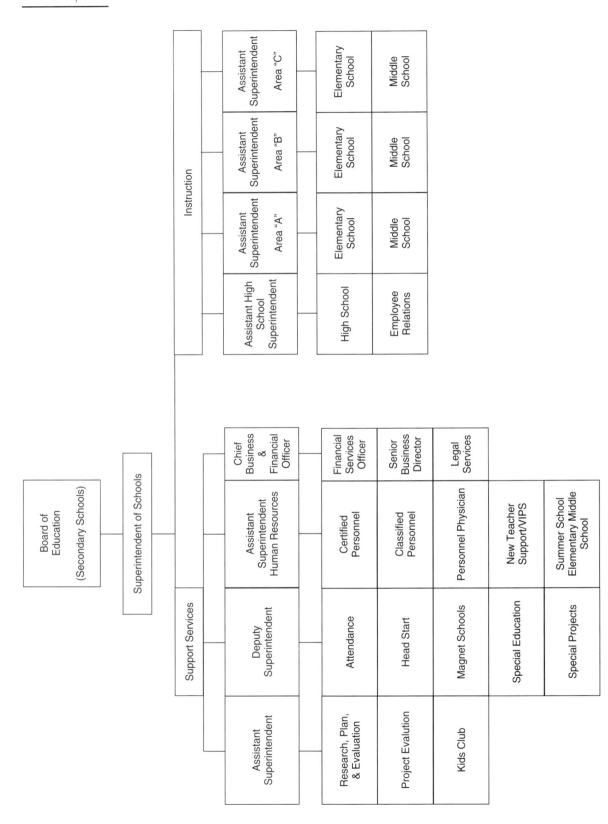

Figure 2.1A *Organizational Chart for Secondary Schools*

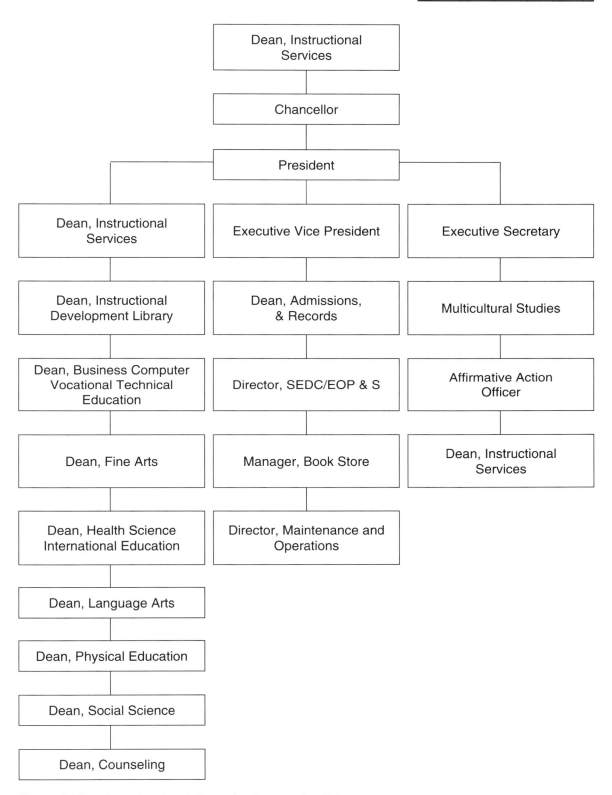

Figure 2.1B   Organizational Chart for Community Colleges

new teachers report that paperwork is one of the two most difficult and frustrating parts of their job—the other being dealing with student discipline problems.

Understanding the Budget

One of the essential things to know is what your budget is. School budgets are prepared in much the same manner as budgets for businesses or the home. The chief administrator is responsible for the entire school's budget, but each entity within the school gets and uses a specific portion. For example, a portion of the budget is earmarked for maintenance (to keep the school plant clean and operable) and another portion is allocated for the purchase of supplies. Each curriculum area (i.e., English, Business, Auto Mechanics, etc.) has a set budget. The department head allocates the money within the department according to the need. For example, once initial equipment purchases have been made, a carpentry program is more expensive to operate than a business skills program and usually receives a larger portion of the budget.

If you are a new teacher it is likely that your budget was set and agreed upon by your predecessor. Any changes for the present year will have to be done administratively. If you are starting a new program, you probably will be given a budget for equipment and supplies to get the program off the ground. The budget and the budget process will be discussed in later chapters as it applies to the particular subject.

Meeting the School Team

To start on the "right foot," extend yourself from the beginning by meeting the other staff and faculty. If you are teaching in a small school, you may be the only one teaching your subject. If so, don't hesitate to call on teachers and building administrators outside your field for assistance in "learning the ropes." Some schools have mentor programs where more experienced teachers volunteer to help new teachers deal with the problems of teaching.

If you are assigned to a medium-to-large school, it is likely that you will find others in your teaching area or related fields. In this situation, a program coordinator or department head can assist you by providing valuable information and general assistance in these important first days.

You will discover that no single teacher or department provides all the education to any one student. Each teacher and person in the school hierarchy is but one member of the team that educates. In the case of schools, the whole is definitely larger than the sum of its parts.

Support Staff

Meeting key school personnel other than teachers and administrators and ensuring their amity and cooperation is essential. A partial list of individuals who can help ensure that your teaching experiences are pleasant is found on the following pages. Don't forget, it is a two-way street—one good favor deserves another. In other words, the best way to ensure continued support is to make sure that you reciprocate and help others in any way possible.

Program or School Secretary.   Anything you can do to make the secretary's job easier will be greatly appreciated. Turn in the required reports and forms, with all the information that was requested, on time. The days of the school secretary who typed all teachers' exams and made and reproduced dittos are long gone, if in fact they ever existed. Today's school secretary is more like an administrative assistant to the principal, responsible for activities that extend well beyond the secretarial. Teachers are expected (especially in these days of computer literacy) to prepare their own tests and instructional materials. Nevertheless, remember the school secretarial staff at special times, such as National Secretary's Week, Valentine's Day, and other holidays. Show that you care; it *does* make a difference.

Professional Resource Staff.   Many school districts have a resource staff available to assist teachers. They can provide a variety of information and materials that will make your job easier. For example, the special education resource person will familiarize you with the needs and requirements of students with disabilities, including implications of the various pieces of legislation pertaining to people with special needs. The curriculum resource person can provide valuable ideas and information on development of your course materials. Counselors can provide assistance regarding career planning for students, testing, and diagnosis. These resource people are there to assist you. Find out what services are available and establish good working relationships with them.

Custodial Staff.   Whether you are assigned a classroom, a laboratory, or both, it is a good policy to establish good working relations with the custodial and maintenance personnel. An excellent idea is to formulate a classroom or laboratory management plan so that routine cleanup and maintenance operations are performed as an integral activity by your classes. Small maintenance tasks that you can accomplish yourself will be greatly appreciated by the maintenance staff. Such activities incorporated as a regular part of instruction also gives the students more of a "real world" experience.

A sound idea is to contact the custodial and maintenance staff soon after you are hired. Work out a cooperative plan so that everyone understands precisely what tasks will be accomplished by whom. Avoiding misunderstandings regarding responsibilities of the custodial and maintenance staff will help ensure a positive working relationship.

Your First Day of Teaching

Now that you have made it through the meetings and getting your facilities ready, you need some advice on how to handle yourself on that first crucial day in front of the class. This section contains some hints on how to deal with some of the more important first-day chores. This section is <u>only</u> an overview (further discussion follows in various chapters). It is important that you prepare for at least the following few things.

Introductions

You have undoubtedly heard the adage that first impressions are the most lasting. It's true. The first impressions that your students have of you (and you of them) could affect the tenor of your class for the entire term, so it's a good idea to "set the stage" from your first meeting.

Students of all ages wonder whether their teachers are really *human*. Let them know who you are, where you have worked, and where you went to school. If you are married and have children, tell them about your family. Do not hesitate to tell your students (in a nonthreatening way, of course) that you are an expert in your field . . . after all, they are there to learn from you.

Experience shows that good teachers are friendly and that their students view them as friends. This does not mean that teachers are or should be *pals, buddies,*

"Actually, this is not my real name, but it should keep any of you from calling me at home!"

4/85

or one of the *homies*. Some teachers write their names on the board as Mr. Smith, or Mrs. Jones, and then tell the students what their first name is. It is rarely a good idea to have students (especially adolescents) call you by your first name.

Course Requirements

From the beginning, let students know what is expected of them in all areas. Give them a syllabus or a list of topics that will be covered in the course, assignments with due dates, and materials, books, and supplies that will be needed. It is essential to tell the students what role you will play in helping them complete the course successfully, what assistance you will provide, and how you will organize the class. Figure 2.2 is an example of a complete course syllabus.

Grading System

Many institutions prescribe the type of grading system that is used. You might even be told how much weight assignments and examinations can have on final grades. For example, many institutions require that grades be based on at least three different types of assessments or demonstrations of competence. Daily assignments might be one area of assessment, projects a second, and exams a third. List the components, criteria, and weights of your grading system in the syllabus or post them in a conspicuous place in the classroom. It is very important that all students know from the outset how they will be graded and what criteria will be used to determine the grade. The elements of a typical grading system may be found in the course syllabus shown in Figure 2.2.

Safety Requirements

Let all students know that safety is of major importance. Explain that safety tests will be administered and that they must be passed prior to the operation of any equipment or machinery. Many school districts have safety tests that are used district-wide for each subject area. Or the school in which you teach may have its own safety regulations. Often, teachers supplement these tests with their own. Tell your students that their safety and that of their peers and the supplies and equipment is of paramount importance, both in class and later on the job. Making this point firmly and unequivocally from the start will save you a lot of grief later on.

Discipline

It would be nice if there were no discipline problems in today's schools. Unfortunately that is not the case. More teachers who leave teaching cite discipline problems as the main reason for quitting. There are numerous ways to maintain order in a classroom, and there are as many books on how to do it (the reference section at the end of this chapter contains some excellent sources). A

Name of Course and Term Here
Institution

Your Name:
Your Office/Classroom Location:
Where and How to Reach You:

Course Description: Place here the "official" description of the course as approved by your educational institution. Students may need this for successive courses they take or for certification requirements.

Course Objectives: Put each of the general course objectives in this section. Go over them on the first day of class as part of the "telling the students what you are going to teach them" activities. Periodically during the course you may need to refer back to these objectives. Place objectives for individual classes on the Instructor's Lesson Plan.

Evaluation Criteria: Describe in this section the criteria that you will use (or that the school requires you to use) in evaluating student progress and achievement. Generally, you will have categories for homework, projects, special assignments, short quizzes, unit examinations, mid-term and final examinations, and attendance and participation. In most instances, you will also provide the numerical scale used for grading. You might also want a section or sentence on the expected student behavior while in class.

Schedule of Classes: This section requires a lot of thought and planning, for here is where you tell the students what they will be learning or studying in class on a day by day basis. If your course meets everyday for one or two hours, you may only show activities on a week by week basis. Provide as much detail as necessary, but do not overdo it. This will serve as your and the students' roadmap to the end of the course.

NOTE: The complete syllabus should not be more than two or three pages in length, but should provide the students with the essential knowlege of what to expect in the course and what is expected of them as students.

Figure 2.2 Elements of a Course Syllabus

complete discussion of discipline is well beyond the scope of this book, but a few pointers may be of help in getting the atmosphere established.

Many discipline problems result from situations where there is a question of control in the classroom. Teacher control is necessary for a number of reasons, but most notably because the school is a place for learning, and learning cannot take place when pandemonium rules. The teacher must exert firm control of the classroom from the moment the students enter. One way to do this is to tell students what is expected of them in terms of behavior, and then be prepared to enforce these rules.

Fortunately, most teachers and students have normal, productive days in school without so much as a threat of violence. Students in occupational programs tend to be older (or more mature) and motivated to be in the class for other reasons, so the tendency for discipline problems or violence in the classroom is lessened. In the event that you ever encounter a threat in the classroom, it is important to <u>not</u> grab or attempt to take a weapon away from a student. Clear the way to an exit so that the student or intruder has a clear exit route. Just as we have fire drills and instruction on what to do during those drills, teachers would be well advised to rehearse other situations as well. In those practice sessions, students should be instructed in the event of violence or the threat of violence to get on the floor and to stay down. These procedures should be practiced with students *before* any violence or threat of violence ever occurs, so that at least one student knows to go get help. Anyone contemplating teaching would be well advised to seek assistance through university classes or self-help books on behavior management. Several such books are found in the reference section at the end of this chapter.

Attendance Procedures

Schools and school systems as well as privately owned schools receive their income on the basis of the numbers of students who are enrolled and in attendance. Most public schools refer to this as ADA (Average Daily Attendance), or FTES (Full-Time Equivalent Students). In addition, teachers are responsible for students who are enrolled in their classes during a given time period. If a student skips a class and is injured or commits a crime while they are enrolled and counted present, the teacher might be held liable. It is imperative that student attendance procedures be set up, maintained, and continuously monitored. Let your students know that attendance is important and that you can't help them learn if they aren't there.

> Many teachers entrust attendance-taking to a student, but because of the legal implications, it is a better practice to do it yourself. Set up a system for attendance-taking; let your students know what it is, and then adhere to it.

Tour

Typically, the first class period with students is spent on introductions and going over paperwork. The last few minutes of the period are well spent conducting a tour of the facility during which you may wish to point out the major pieces of equipment, safety zones, material storage, fire protection equipment, exits, and first aid materials. Use this opportunity to stress the safety aspects of your facility and which areas are off-limits until safety tests have been passed.

Settling-In Activities

Once you are hired, you should begin to assess your surroundings. Some suggestions about how you might deal with these surroundings and some ideas on getting started are presented in this section. If you are fortunate, you will have several days or even weeks to prepare for these "settling-in activities." Review this information again after that monumental first day of teaching.

Preparation of a Safe Classroom and Laboratory

The phrase "safety first" is especially important for beginning teachers. Competent teaching and thorough preparation of curriculum mean little if serious accidents occur in your facility. Seasoned teachers (particularly those unfortunate enough to have experienced accidents) agree that safety is one of a teacher's most important responsibilities. Federal legislation has done much to ensure that states conform to minimum safety practices in both industrial and school settings. It is, therefore, extremely important that you understand your responsibilities under federal, state, and local regulations and that you take immediate steps to develop a complete safety plan as a component of your curriculum. Below are some guidelines to consider when preparing your safety program. Remember, however, that your individual responsibilities for safety *must* come from your particular teaching situation. If you are not sure of your specific local and state regulations, check with your immediate supervisor or state department of education personnel. Most states have safety information available for teachers to use in the classroom. The following areas merit your particular attention.

Tools, Machinery, and Equipment. Start your safety program by initiating a thorough performance and safety inspection of *each* piece of tooling, machinery, and equipment that is assigned to you *before* allowing students to operate them. Specifically, check for the following:

- Appropriate guards and protective devices
- Correct wiring practices (approved code for school facilities)
- Worn parts that could create a safety hazard
- Machines and equipment that should be anchored to the floor or a bench
- Adequate spacing and placement of equipment to ensure safety for students during operation

- Safety zones maintained around machines
- Hand and power tools that are sharp, safe, and clean
- Danger zones that are adequately marked
- Any lifting or hoisting equipment is in safe working condition
- Machines meet noise level requirements when being operated

Once classes begin, your safety checks for machinery and tools should include:

- Assurance that all machines are off when not in use
- Supervision of all tools and machines when being operated
- Assurance that all machines and power tools are *off* when the instructor is not present
- Classrooms should always be maintained in such order that they could pass a surprise check by the fire department or other government or insurance agency.

Student Safety.   Students enrolled in your classes are entrusted to your supervision while they are in your facility. This responsibility cannot be taken lightly. A new teacher should obtain all safety information available concerning policies for students enrolled in both classroom and shop or laboratory courses. Federal legislation mandates that states comply with strict enforcement of personal safety codes and regulations in both industry and education. At the local level, building administrators and teachers are given the ultimate responsibility for maintaining safety programs.

What does this mean to you as a beginning teacher? The information presented here as well as information obtained from local, state, and federal sources should be used to carefully develop your own personal safety program and implement it throughout your curriculum. You will also want to cover these topics.

1. Current methods of using tools, instruments, and machines
2. Appropriate clothing and hair protection
3. Eye protection including safety glasses and protective shields
4. Student reporting of hazardous situations
5. Correct lifting procedures
6. Correct use of compressed air
7. Horseplay rules
8. Respect for electrical devices
9. Policies regarding jewelry, including rings, clips, and chains
10. Proper use and care of respirators used in dusty or toxic conditions
11. Ear protection devices

Other concepts of safety that may be specific to your class should also be considered.

Facility-Related Safety.   The best rule here is simply "cover the waterfront," meaning that you should check every building-related safety item. Here are two examples.

1. Fire Extinguishers
   a. *Hand Held.* First, check the date to determine whether the certification is valid. Also, read the directions carefully and commit the operating procedure to memory. Familiarize your students with the process. Check local regulations for extinguisher locations within your facility. A check by the local fire department is free and is your best single source of information on additional fire safety questions.
   b. *Sprinkler and Heat Sensitive Systems.* These systems are often maintained by the installer or district maintenance personnel. Periodic inspection is necessary, but they require little or no maintenance. Check your local regulations.

2. Barrier-Free Exits
   All fire exits must be properly marked, usually with lighted exit signs, and be free from any machinery, equipment, supplies, or other hindrances. Make sure that you also provide a barrier-free runway to the fire doors. Doors should swing out and be fitted with a safety bar if possible.

Fire Plan. Your school undoubtedly has a comprehensive fire plan that includes your facility. Check the plan carefully; then develop a comprehensive fire drill procedure for each class. Make sure your students understand it and can execute a quick and orderly exit.

Heating and Cooling System. Familiarize yourself with the type of heating and cooling system furnished for your facility. If the system is exposed (such as suspended space heaters) or could in any way cause a fire or heat-related accident, take necessary precautions.

First-Aid Certification. Most states require that persons teaching classes in which accidents may occur must possess a valid first-aid card. If you are not first-aid qualified, become so as quickly as possible. Check your first-aid kit station and ensure that it is well stocked with the necessary items. If you are not sure what the kit should contain, check with your supervisor, the district office, or the kit manufacturer. Teachers, particularly teachers of adults, also are well advised to have Cardiopulmonary Resuscitation (CPR) certification, and many states now require such certification as a condition of credential renewal.

Accident Reporting Procedures. Learn the accident reporting procedures adopted by your school. If possible, set up a file with all the necessary forms and a procedural outline. Follow it carefully! Keep copies of all records for future reference and for your own protection. Figure 2.3 contains a sample accident reporting form. If your school has no such form, use the elements of this form when reporting accidents.

TO BE COMPLETED IMMEDIATELY!

The school employee who either witnesses the student injury or is supervising the student at the time of the injury should complete this form. If possible, the report should be submitted immediately to the administrator's office. Should other pertinent facts develop, notify the administrator's office by means of a supplemental report.

This report is for the confidential use of the insurance company and of attorney's for the school and its employees in defending litigation

ACCIDENT/INCIDENT REPORT FORM			

SCHOOL

SCHOOL ADDRESS	PHONE	

STUDENT'S NAME	AGE	GRADE

HOME ADDRESS		PHONE

WHERE DID ACCIDENT OCCUR?	DATE	TIME

HOW DID ACCIDENT OCCUR?

NATURE OF INJURY?

FIRST AID APPLIED? yes__ no__	BY WHOM?	DISPOSITION OF INJURED STUDENT (RETURN TO CLASS, HOME, DOCTOR, HOSPITAL)

DOES INJURED STUDENT HAVE SCHOOL ACCIDENT INSURANCE COVERAGE? yes__ no__	NAME OF INSURANCE COMPANY

WAS ANY SCHOOL RULE VIOLATED? yes__ no__	IF SO EXPLAIN, COMMENT ON SUPERVISION

WITNESSES AT TIME OF ACCIDENT: NAME:	ADDRESS:	PHONE:

HAVE PARENTS CONTACTED SCHOOL? IF YES, EXPLAIN BELOW. yes__ no__	WERE PARENTS CONTACTED BY SCHOOL? IF YES, EXPLAIN BELOW. yes__ no__	WERE PARENTS OR STUDENT TOLD THEY WOULD BE CONTACTED AGAIN? (EXPLAIN BELOW) yes__ no__

COMMENTS:

REPORT SUBMITTED BY	POSITION	DATE	ADMINISTRATOR	DATE

Figure 2.3 Accident/incident Report

Facility Ventilation.   If you work in any facility that produces agents such as smoke, sawdust, or potentially toxic fumes, check the ventilation system carefully. Determine that the system is functioning properly and is being maintained regularly.

Lighting.   Poor lighting conditions can contribute to serious accidents. Use an appropriate light metering device to ensure that you have adequate lighting for reading, machine operation, and mixing of chemicals.

Fluorescent lighting is commonly used to illuminate school facilities. It is an excellent system providing even, functional lighting. A word of caution: Because of the way it operates (it flickers), certain moving objects such as running saw blades, milling cutters, or mixers can actually appear at certain RPM. to be motionless. Test this condition in your facility. If this situation occurs, you should establish appropriate policies to *prevent accidents.*

Laboratory Capacity.   A frequently overlooked safety hazard is an overcrowded facility. Check the number of work stations or seats in your facility and determine how many students you can safely work with at any one time. Then check state, district, or school policy regarding enrollments. Work closely with your department chairperson or building administrator to ensure that the class enrollments are compatible with safe instruction.

Safety Implications for Students with Disabilities.   You have an important obligation as a teacher to make sure that students with disabilities enrolled in your classes are provided the same educational opportunities as all of the other students. Special considerations such as barrier-free classes or laboratories must be provided. Be aware that you may have to make certain changes to your facility to accommodate the safety of these students. For example, such items as fire extinguishers, first-aid kits, and fire alarms must be mounted low enough for wheelchair access. Many of these changes can be accommodated quickly and inexpensively. Funds also are available through federal or state programs to help schools prepare for meeting the special needs of some students. Contact your immediate supervisor or building administrator for assistance if students with disabilities are enrolled.

Teacher Liability in the Classroom or Laboratory.   It is important that you fully understand your responsibility and liabilities as a teacher in the class and laboratory. Most school systems provide some type of partial or total liability insurance for teachers. In many districts insurance coverage is the responsibility of the teacher association. Other school systems provide a basic policy as part of employee-employer benefits. In addition, the various professional associations (such as the American Vocational Association) offer liability insurance plans.

As a new teacher, you should determine your personal liability in case of an accident in your facility, and then take positive steps to ensure that you (as an individual) have adequate protection.

Security of the Facility

The security of your assigned area is fundamental to successful teaching. The first person you typically see about security is the head custodian who has the necessary keys to your facility. After you have been issued keys, survey your assigned teaching area and develop a security plan. This plan is nothing more than a formal system of accounting for *all* aspects of securing your facility, from student lockers to windows. Many teachers develop a comprehensive management plan for their facility with students playing a major contributing role. For example, security arrangements can be established so that a comprehensive security check can be accomplished at the end of each class period. Some important security factors that you should be aware of are:

Doors and Windows. Develop a means of determining that all windows are both lockable and tamperproof. Then check them each time you leave the facility.

Student Project Storage. This area or room should be lockable, and no one should have access unless you are present. Depending on the subject taught and the size of the projects, shelves, lockers, or cabinets should be provided to keep student items safe from theft or tampering.

Your Office. Tests, grade books, student records, computers, books, and other valuable materials are commonly located in your office. Make sure your office door can be secured and develop a policy that covers the appropriateness of students being in the office. It is usually a good idea to make your desk off-limits to students at all times.

Security of Small Tools and Instruments

Without a full complement of tools and equipment, your program cannot be operated effectively. To prevent loss or theft, try the following suggestions.

Tools and Precision Instruments. A variety of methods can be used to secure these expensive items. Many teachers find that open storage areas are appropriate when the main facility is secured properly. A second method is to place easily lost items in secured cabinets or drawers within the room or laboratory. A third, and perhaps the most secure and easily managed storage system, is an area or room that is used expressly for issuance and general storage of tools, instruments, and supplies. Commonly called the tool room or tool crib in industry, this is one of the best and most secure storage and accounting systems.

Select the system you find most appropriate, but be aware that you should not place yourself or your students in the position of compromising your program because of damaged or missing items. In other words, it is absolutely necessary to develop a relatively foolproof system of accounting for items necessary to offer a comprehensive and high-quality program.

Student Lockers.   Many schools provide student lockers in the classroom or laboratory. Whether it is storage of clothing, materials, or supplies, it is important to develop a system that provides real security for students' personal items. Typical storage accommodations include lockers, shelving areas, drawers, or cabinets. For each system, it is important to ensure that each storage area is lockable and that *you* control the system.

Organization of Your Administrative Area (Office)

Many schools provide an office or administrative area where teachers can organize paperwork, plan lessons, and counsel students. Some of the things you will have or need in your office are discussed in the following paragraphs.

File Cabinet.   A file cabinet is useful for organizing curriculum materials, tests, student records, evaluation forms, and handouts. If student records are stored in the file cabinet, it should be locked at all times when you are not present.

Computer and Media Storage.   Computer software, CD-ROM, paper, and printer ribbons or cartridges should be kept in one secure area. Most schools have site licenses for computer software that restrict the number of machines that it can be installed on. The integrity of the site license agreement is only protected by maintaining a secure storage facility for the software. It is also a good idea to restrict access to the computer itself by using a password or other security system.

Desk.   A desk in your administrative area provides a convenient place to do paperwork. Most desks can be locked, so your desk can provide storage for small but valuable tools and instruments. Student records may also be stored in a locked desk.

Book Shelves.   Beg, build, or borrow enough book shelves to hold your texts, periodicals, and reference materials. You may wish to set up one section as a student resource center. If students will have access to reference materials, set up a checkout system so you know who has your materials.

Telephone.   If you teach in a laboratory or classroom where accidents may occur, the installation of a telephone not only makes sense, but in some states is mandatory. In an emergency, a telephone provides immediate access to aid. It is important to secure the telephone so that it may not be mis-used.

Student Counseling Area.   Organize your office so that it lends itself to student counseling. You will be talking privately to students more than you may think. It is important to establish the right environment, as this is a major function of teaching. You can do this by providing chairs (preferably next to, not across from, your desk) and assuring that voices are not carried into the classroom or laboratory.

Ordering Materials, Supplies, and Equipment

A third important task is the ordering of necessary supplies, materials, services, and text books. Most expendable materials, such as wood, steel, bandages, paint, and paper should be ordered immediately because delivery to your facility typically takes several days or even weeks.

Textbook Ordering

You must decide whether your classes require text materials. If so, you may encounter one of two situations. On one hand, you may inherit a set of existing texts. If they will suffice for the first class period (i.e., quarter, semester, or year), then you can simply use them and order new ones at your convenience. Some proprietary schools have a preestablished curriculum and books, in which event you will not be able to change these texts. If, on the other hand, the existing books are not appropriate or if no books exist, then you must get permission to submit a priority requisition and order new books. In most instances the matter will be handled through the district offices. However, you can ensure that your order receives priority by hand-carrying the necessary paperwork through the system. A number of factors must be considered when ordering textbooks. A form that will help you identify those that are most applicable to your situation may be found in the appendix.

If you find the books won't be in for several weeks, ask permission of the publisher or copyright holder to duplicate necessary materials from your own copy. Do this by contacting the copyright owner or the owner's authorized agent—they will usually be named in the formal copyright notice on the original work, or by contacting the Copyright Clearance Center on the World Wide

"I'm taking an innovative approach to teaching this semester. I'm using books!"

2/78

Web at web address **http://www.copyright.com**. Be prepared to provide the proposed use of the material and why you need to copy it. Although oral permissions are generally legally valid, it is always best to document the permission with a letter that the grantor will sign and return to you.

A second way to solve the problem of not having sufficient text material on hand is to place your copy of duplicated materials on a two-hour reserve in the school library. Each student then has access to the text. This, of course, places the students at a serious inconvenience by having to wait for the material and not being able to study at their leisure.

Services

It is easy to overlook essential services needed to make your class run smoothly. Making sure these services start prior to the first day of classes or as soon as possible thereafter will enable you to concentrate on more important items like keeping the class running and maintaining your sanity! Some of the more important services are:

Custodial Services. Seasoned teachers generally agree that it is easier to work in a classroom or laboratory that is clean and orderly. Typical custodial services include maintenance of floors, the work area, benches and tables, waste containers, windows, and lights. In an era of fiscal cutbacks, custodial services are often the first to be cut. Use your students to maintain their own work areas and the floors as much as possible. They will need to do this later on the job, so the classroom is the best place to develop the habit.

Electricity, Gas, Water, and Telephone. Energy conservation often means discontinuing these services during nonschool periods. Check with your supervisor to ensure that you will have these when you need them.

Materials and Supplies

It is difficult to teach computer applications without floppy disks and printer paper! Similarly, for most technical courses, both expendable and nonexpendable items are necessary. As a new teacher, it is a good idea to "over organize" the first time around. Simply stated, this means that the sooner you determine which materials you need and have them ordered, the better. Many items may be available locally within one or two days. However, if you teach in a rural location or a large metropolitan district, you may wait weeks or months for some items. To further complicate the situation, many school districts have regulations stipulating that certain materials be acquired only through the competitive bid process. Remember, too, that supply houses often are hard pressed to fill school orders promptly during summer months, since that period is when they receive the most orders. In the following year, you can eliminate the problems by (1) staggering your orders throughout the year, or (2) submitting your orders early and maintaining a stock of needed items.

Initial Course Planning

A seemingly formidable task for any new teacher is determining how to organize course materials. There is usually little time to organize or develop course materials *before* you start that first day of teaching. Here are some ideas on how you can survive until you have time to sit down, take a breath, and identify some concrete course goals, objectives, student activities, and evaluation materials.

Start by asking other teachers, administrators, or your department head if there are approved curriculum materials available. You may be lucky and find that the courses you will teach are part of a well-articulated school or state curriculum effort. If this is the case, you most likely will find a curriculum guide with specific course information including goals, objectives, class/laboratory learning activities, tests, and perhaps even daily lesson plans.

Another possibility is to locate materials developed by the teacher who previously taught your assigned courses. You may find a complete guide and syllabus, or at least a minimum of materials to get you started.

A third possibility is to talk with other teachers in the district or adjoining districts who teach the same or similar courses. They will most likely share ideas and even materials with you. Remember that help is a two-way street. Devise a way to return their assistance.

Your state department of education may help in your search for curriculum materials. States typically have recommended or approved curriculum materials available. Write or call the person in charge of your curriculum area for assistance.

College and universities with teacher preparation programs will often maintain a file of curriculum guides for most subject areas in the library or a curriculum resource center. They may also have materials from other states.

While on the topic of colleges and universities, you may wish to check with the faculty of undergraduate and graduate programs in your subject field. These departments usually maintain excellent files of curriculum materials developed by students as part of teacher preparation and graduate programs.

Local community advisory committees can also provide you with valuable information on initial curriculum development. This group typically works closely with teachers and can provide knowledgeable information on community needs and available resources.

It is likely that you simply will not have the time or the experience at this point in your teaching career to develop a complete set of course materials before you begin teaching. In fact, it is recommended that you *not* try to develop too much too soon. Start with a basic framework for the course, then plan on continually modifying, rewriting, and adding details based on meetings with advisory groups, student input, development of your own teaching style, and general teaching experience. Once you have identified the essential components of the course framework, it is relatively easy to develop a more complete course guide.

The first and most important component of the framework is the set of major goals for each course. For example, a major goal of many courses is that students will develop enough skill and knowledge to survive in an entry-level job. Consult with school personnel, the state office and advisory groups, and/or program administrators to be sure that you are placing the proper emphasis on the course. Chapter 5 contains a discussion of how curriculum is developed for the occupational class.

The second component of your curriculum framework is the specific performance or behavioral objectives written for each major course goal. The third component is the development of student learning activities. These include the things the students will do in class in order to master the competencies that are specified in the performance objectives.

The fourth component of developing the curriculum is to identify teaching methods or strategies that you, the teacher, will incorporate in the classroom in order to help the students master the necessary competencies that were identified in the performance objectives. The fifth component you will need to identify early is the material you will need to teach the course.

Last, but certainly of great importance, are the ways you will evaluate the following: (1) student learning, (2) your teaching effectiveness, and (3) the course curriculum.

As you can see, once the basic goals are identified, it is necessary to sequentially follow up by writing objectives, learning activities, and so on. Remember, too, that it isn't necessary to assemble the entire course framework during these first few days or weeks. Identification of the major course goals and enough specific objectives and learning activities for a one-to-two week period are sufficient. You will have a much better idea on how to proceed after you have spent two or three weeks in the classroom.

How then do you develop the more complete curriculum materials for each course? A full explanation of how to develop a course guide, including examples of goals, objectives, and learning activities is covered in Chapter 5.

Professional Involvement

Teaching, whether it is in public and private schools, or in industry, will require at least some involvement with various professional organizations and associations. This involvement can be beneficial to your career development and ultimately to your students.

As a new teacher, you will probably hear many differing opinions about teachers' associations, youth leadership development organizations, advisory groups, and professional educational associations. It is in your best interest to examine each opinion carefully. Most of these organizations and associations serve different, but important, purposes.

Here are some hints for evaluating organizations and associations:

- Talk with several colleagues (teachers and administrators).
- Read the recruitment literature.
- Determine the organization's or association's mission or purpose.

- Ask yourself; What can I give to the organization? What can I gain from membership?
- How much time and money can I afford?

Remember, you are joining a profession, education, and yet you want to maintain a commitment to your technical field. Many teachers select several organizations that provide opportunities for both technical and professional involvement.

Let's now turn to five types of organizations: teachers' associations, teachers' unions, youth leadership development organizations, advisory groups, and professional education associations.

Teachers' Associations

Not so many years ago many school districts required, or strongly urged, that teachers belong to the local teachers' association. Membership typically includes affiliation with the state teachers' association and the National Education Association. Teachers' associations usually have strong, professional interests and services. These interests and services include:

- A code of ethics
- Professional literature for personal and classroom use
- Active support for legislation at the local, state, and national levels
- Insurance programs, including professional liability protection.

Teachers' Unions

Teachers' unions began to rapidly expand their membership in the 1960s. Their growth was due in great part to a need for much stronger job security and appropriate salary increases. Working primarily through the collective bargaining process, unions have often been able to meet their objectives. In response to union activity, teachers' associations have also begun to work through collective bargaining.

The formal and informal battles between several teachers' associations' members have been bitter in some school districts. This atmosphere may exist in your district or school. Assess the situation carefully before you join either organization. Remember, however, that both groups have their strong points; and, if you join, choose the group that will, in your opinion, support professional growth and security.

Youth Leadership

You have undoubtedly heard of youth leadership groups such as Junior Achievement and 4-H. Their goals and activities are generally well known. In the public and private schools, there are similar groups that are an important part of the school's curriculum. Their existence depends on strong teacher support *and* participation.

These groups help students gain the skills, knowledge, and attitudes necessary to live in a working world. Students are given the opportunity to take leadership and followership roles, and through these roles gain confidence and recognition from their peers, teachers, and parents.

Some of the well-known student leadership development organizations include:

- Business Professionals of America (office education)
- DECA, Distributive Education Clubs of America (marketing education)
- FBLA/Phi Beta Lambda (business leadership)
- National FFA Organization (agriculture)
- Future Homemakers of America/HERO (consumer and home economics)
- Health Occupations Students of America (health care)
- National Postsecondary Agricultural Student Organization
- National Young Farmers Education Association (adult students in agriculture)
- Technology Student Association (high-skill technology)
- VICA, Vocational Industrial Clubs of America (skill training and leadership)

What will your decision be if you are asked by your principal or department chairperson to become faculty advisor to one of the school's youth leadership groups? What will you do if some of your students ask you to help out? Remember, teaching entails more than five or six periods a day. Addresses of the several student organizations may be found in the appendix.

Advisory Groups

Advisory committees are important to the proper functioning of many educational programs. When used well, they can be an invaluable resource.

Advisory committees are used by schools and other educational and training institutions to provide input from community, business, industry, and government. Schools often will have an advisory board to ensure that the community has an input to the operation and offerings of the school. These committees may be made up of parents, students, business leaders, governmental officials, religious leaders, and other interested parties.

Similar committees are used to advise and support vocational education programs. These committees represent the business and job community. When used effectively, they can provide critical information on the latest developments in your field including technological changes, changing job requirements, and job market demand. Many advisory board members are a source for equipment, materials, supplies, and jobs for students. This key group is typically comprised of (1) business and industrial leaders, (2) skilled craft people, and (3) union or governmental officials.

It is *vitally important* that you understand and effectively use your advisory committees. There are many people in your community who feel strongly about the value of education and who are eager for the opportunity to participate.

Professional Associations

One of the real problems of the educational profession is the generally poor involvement by teachers in their various professional associations. Probably the first comment you will hear from your colleagues is, What has the association done for me? It is a difficult question to answer because many who ask do so with a closed mind; that is, they do not want to join anyway.

Some of these associations, such as the National Education Association and the American Vocational Association, continually fight for legislation that makes your job *possible*. Literally thousands of teachers would not be able to provide valuable educational services had these associations not been in Washington, DC, promoting the type of programs you are or will be teaching.

These organizations provide more than just legislative support. They keep their members up-to-date on educational issues and trends. They provide special services such as legal advice and insurance programs. Many hold regular conventions at which the profession meets to establish operating policies, review vendors' products and services, and exchange ideas on their various programs.

Take time to review the several organizations in your field. Join those that you feel will help you *and* the profession. The dues for these organizations are generally tax deductible. Addresses of the largest and most active associations may be found in the appendix.

Summary

The first few days of teaching are an overwhelming experience. There are, however, many ways to make the transition into teaching as painless as possible. One of the most critical areas of concern for the new teacher of vocational subjects is safety.

Safety is a serious matter. As a new teacher, you should use every resource available to become thoroughly familiar with all federal, state, and local safety regulations concerning your teaching area. Many resources are available for gathering this information, including: (1) federal regulations; (2) state policy guidelines; (3) state department of education printed materials; (4) local district or building safety guides; and (5) commercially available materials including those available from the National Safety Council. Safety should be an integral part of each vocational curriculum. The safety program should contain information on general facility safety; tools, machinery, and equipment considerations; personal (student) safety; special consideration for students with disabilities; and security measures.

Your personal safety and liability as a teacher warrants your special attention. The best policy regarding safety in the classroom is to develop an excellent safety program. You are then in a position to maintain a "zero accident" approach.

Organizations and associations are important to you, your profession, and ultimately your students. As a teacher, your job requires more than just teaching a few classes: it requires you to be involved. You will be a better educator if you actively support the various educational organizations and associations.

For Further Reading

Alschuler, A.S. (1980). *School Discipline: A Socially Literate Solution.* New York: McGraw-Hill Book Company.

Charles, C.M. (1996). *Building Classroom Discipline.* (Fifth Edition). White Plains, NY: Longman.

Gathercoal, F., and Stern, S. (1987). *Legal Issues for Industrial Educators.* Ann Arbor, MI: Prakken Publications.

Johnson, S.O. (1980). *Better Discipline: A Practical Approach.* Springfield, IL: Charles C. Thomas, Publisher.

Kigin, D.J. (1987). *Teacher Liability in School-Shop Accidents.* Ann Arbor, MI: Prakken Publications.

Kohurt, S., Jr. (1986). *Classroom Discipline: Case Studies and Viewpoints.* Second Edition. Washington, DC: National Education Association.

"Let's Teach Safety: A Directory of Classroom Resources." (1980). Joint Safety Committee of the American Vocational Association and the National Safety Council. Washington, DC: American Vocational Association.

National School Boards Association (1993). *Violence in the Schools.* Alexandria, VA: National School Boards Association.

Schloss, P.J. (1994). *Applied Behavior Analysis in the Classroom.* Boston: Allyn & Bacon.

Sprick, R.S. (1985). *Discipline in the Secondary Classroom: A Problem-by-Problem Survival Guide.* West Nyack, NY: The Center for Applied Research in Education.

Exercises

Using the examples in Figure 2.1, create an organization chart for the school or agency where you work. Follow the hierarchy, or chain of command as it exists. Place all names, correct titles, and telephone extensions in the chart so that you may use it for reference later.

3 How People Learn

Some Principles of Learning

PEOPLE DO NOT LEARN by having knowledge funneled into their heads. People *do* learn by using all of their senses. People learn because they want to and because they have to. Sometimes, people learn in spite of the instruction they receive. Reasons for learning and the styles or manners by which people learn are as varied and as multifaceted as snowflakes. This chapter contains a short discussion of learning theories, a number of principles of learning that are believed to be universal, and some hints on how to incorporate them in classroom instruction. A number of student learning styles or peculiarities are discussed, as are some of the many differences that occupational education students bring to the classroom.

Learning Theories

The principles of learning that are described in this chapter are drawn from four major categories of theories about learning: *motivation, transfer, retention, and reinforcement.* Many teacher candidates will ask, Why should I study learning principles?, or, Why should I understand all of these theories?

Almost every job requires that the person who performs it understand the principles that support or are relevant to the tasks required. The principles that are relevant will vary from task to task. For an automobile mechanic, the principles of the internal combustion engine are important; for a legislative advocate, an understanding of how the committee system of Congress was established and works is important. If these people fail to understand important principles, their jobs will be much harder; they will not be able to build their knowledge; and their effectiveness will be impaired. Principles of learning and their application are among the most important things that a teacher should master. Such knowledge will help teachers to function more effectively in whatever classroom situations they find themselves.

An understanding of how people learn is particularly important for those who are interested in providing improved instruction. An understanding of learning principles will help the teacher establish conditions in a classroom that will make it easier for students to attain new skills and knowledge and develop appropriate attitudes toward work. This is why there is an emphasis on instructional techniques and strategies in courses in teacher preparation programs. The preparation of good lesson plans, the provision of demonstrations and appropriate learning materials, and the allowance for opportunities to practice new skills are among many applications of learning principles. And the applications do not stop at the classroom door but are carried over into home life and social situations, such as when we raise children and work in the community.

Teachers of occupational subjects will be able to develop materials, design curricula, and plan instruction if they understand and are able to apply the principles of learning.

Definitions of Learning

Psychologists and educators have argued over the details of definitions of *learning* for generations and show every sign of continuing the dispute well into the future. These disagreements notwithstanding, most now agree that an event of learning includes a *relatively permanent change* that can be *observed in the behavior* of a person that comes about as a *result of interaction with the environment*. This definition has important implications for curriculum development, for classroom instruction, and for assessing learning.

First, learning is *relatively permanent*. While the possibility must be allowed that someone might forget something eventually, it cannot be said that someone has really learned something unless it is retained for later use. This is important, as occupational education is designed to help people perform on the job, not just in class. The whole purpose of occupational education is to prepare the students to perform on the job after they leave school. Therefore, teachers must be concerned that the students retain what they are supposed to learn.

Second, what is learned should be *observable in the person's behavior*. This is another way of saying that people must be able to apply what they have learned. It is as true for attitudes as for knowledge and motor skills. Whatever it is that we are trying to teach, we should be able to see, through students' behavior, that they have acquired it and are able to demonstrate it. Some changes in behavior come about by the process of aging or other factors and are not really learned, but are instead responses to physiological phenomena such as illness, fatigue, or the effects of substances. Behavior in such instances is not the result of learning as defined here.

Finally, the behavioral change that is observed is the *result of contacts with the environment*. This excludes changes that occur naturally as the learner matures. Related to this is the important point that some "contacts" are more effective than others. For example, a student may be better able to follow correct safety procedures in the classroom and on the job if these procedures are demonstrated rather than just described.

Learning Concepts and the Teacher

Teachers of occupational subjects wish their students to gain a wide variety of skills, knowledge, and attitudes. An understanding of learning principles will help the teacher to gear instruction so that each student can reach these goals. It will also help in providing effective instruction and diagnosing learning difficulties when problems arise.

Notice that the preceding statement says that understanding learning principles will *help* the teacher, not that they will solve the teacher's problems. Learning principles are tools that must be used with skill; they will no more solve problems than hammers will drive nails. Each tool must be used skillfully. Moreover, knowledge of learning principles can never substitute for a thorough understanding of the occupational subject area. Such principles can help the teacher transmit skills, knowledge, and attitudes more effectively, but the teacher must first be thoroughly competent in the subject. The four major categories of learning theories are discussed in the following paragraphs.

Motivation Theories.   When teachers attempt to motivate students, they are attempting to arouse the students' interest in the subject matter and, not incidentally, the teaching itself. The theories regarding motivation are an attempt to explain why and how individuals become interested in doing something. The two extremes of the motivation theories as they are applied to education were borrowed from other disciplines, most notably psychology and management. Classroom teachers tend to develop their own motivation practices based on their knowledge of the research and the subject, their personal characteristics, and the characteristics of the students. A motivation theory and its accompanying practice that works in one situation might not work in another situation or with a different group of learners. The basic thing to remember at this point about motivation (and the thing that has the most practical significance for teachers) is that without motivation, students will learn only with much difficulty. One of the teacher's roles is to find out what motivates the students and then use that knowledge to get them interested in learning the subject at hand. If students are not aware of a need to learn, or if they cannot see the relevance of learning for their personal use, they will not learn, or at most, their learning will be transitory and therefore functionally useless.

Transfer of Learning Theories.   The true test of teaching is the permanence of the learning that results. The long-range effect of an instructional situation is the essence of transfer of learning. There are different types of transfer to be considered. Skill areas require a transfer that allows the learner to retain a necessary skill level to the degree that provides automatic performance, such as touch typing, hammering, and basic skills. Attitude areas require a transfer that allows for forgetting total content, but retention of the overall attitude. An example of this might be safety attitudes associated with the use of a particular tool that becomes outdated and is replaced with a newer and different tool. Transfer, then, is the adaptation of specific skills or attitudes from original situations to other situations.

Early approaches to transfer of learning were based upon the notion that the learning of difficult subjects such as Latin and geometry would improve the learning ability in general. From this attitude of learning purely for the sake of learning, the pendulum swung toward the attitude that learning should be only for real-life situations, and only material that the students will use daily should be taught. John Dewey and others during the 1920s and 1930s were the chief proponents of this idea. Today, educators favor the teaching of general principles, ideas, and approaches to problem solving since these areas comprise the types of learning that are thought to be most susceptible to transfer. Applying this concept, teachers encourage the student to make individual applications of material as the need arises. The students are then shown the potential usefulness of principles, so when conditions that call for their use arise, they will remember the information and will know how to apply it. A basic premise of the transfer theory is that students must use information if they are to remember it. Practice in using a concept or a piece of equipment is, therefore, essential for transfer to take place.

Transfer of the original learning to other situations can be positive or negative depending upon the degree and direction of the generalized stimulus. Numerous studies have shown that the amount of transfer will vary with the students' ages, grade level, subject matter, the form in which the material was presented, and with the direction of transfer, whether horizontal, as within a sequence of courses, or vertical, such as from one subject to another. Transfer is an accepted phenomenon, but the how and why of its occurrence are still not totally understood.

In order for transfer to take place, certain conditions must be met.

1. The basic principles of the material to be studied must be isolated and their importance as an area of study must be made clear to and be accepted by the students. In other words, the students need to know what they are going to study and why it is important.

2. The students must practice or apply the new principles to similar situations, then to more remote situations later in order to learn, as well as reduce the possibility of forgetting, the information.

3. The students need to practice the principle in nonclass-related situations and must encounter situations to which the principle is not applicable so that they will understand when to use and when not to use the information.

When developing a curriculum, the teacher must provide for practice and reapplication of skills or knowledge that are taught so that the students can learn and be able to use the content of the course. The role of the teacher, then, is to ensure that adequate opportunity is given the student to learn and apply the principles presented in class.

Retention Theories. Retention theories are concerned with how what is learned is remembered. Retention permits establishment of a relationship with other events and the transfer of data to new situations. Studies have shown that when facts are learned, as a general rule, three-fourths of the facts will still be remembered by the end of the course; one-half of the facts will be remembered by the end of the following year; and only one-fourth of the facts by the end of the second year. In other words, people forget approximately 80 percent of all facts learned in a course within a two-year period. In order to improve this percentage, the teacher should keep general retention theory research findings in mind when preparing the curriculum.

It has been found that meaningful information also includes those facts, generalizations, rules, and principles that the student considers useful.

Teachers must select appropriate course content and then help the students identify its applicability to their own situations. Material that is learned with insight, or understanding, is likely to be permanent and can become a part of the individual's learning structure. On the other hand, people tend to forget unpleasant and unimportant pieces of data. This fact helps explain why otherwise capable students often do so poorly on examinations that test trivial facts.

Many years of study have indicated that five factors facilitate retention.

1. An individual's personality
2. Meaningfulness of the information, or knowledge of how it can be used
3. The order of presentation of the material to be learned
4. Thorough mastery of the subject obtained through practice and application
5. Review of the information through the use of tests and other evaluations

The most important of these factors is the so-called personal dynamic complex of the people themselves: their interests, intentions, and attitudes all influence what they will remember from any subject presented in class. Meaningful information is that which has meaningful content and approach; rote-learned or memorized material is not usually retained much beyond the final examination. The order of presentation, or organization, implies that data to be learned should be presented so that like concepts are grouped and related to each other (preferably in a unit of instruction) rather than presented as groups of unrelated bits of information. Thorough mastery of a subject requires that students have enough practice of the subject matter so that they will not forget the material learned during a period of nonlearning or nonpractice. Review reduces the possibility of forgetting material and can restore forgotten material to memory. Periodic testing is an effective method of reviewing earlier-learned concepts and skills. It is especially effective when students are given the opportunity to confirm the accuracy of their answers or to learn the correct response. Teachers should keep this in mind when developing tests. Cumulative tests are especially effective because they permit the student to review earlier-learned materials. The most effective method of review might be to allow the students time and opportunity to use earlier-learned concepts throughout the course. Whenever possible, test construction should be part of the development of a unit of instruction. This is covered in greater depth in Chapter 7.

Activities designed to improve retention can be incorporated into the curriculum. Teachers must be aware of factors influencing retention so that they can provide proper direction for their students. Remember that retention is a very personal trait that can be guided through directed and spaced practice and presentation of material, but ultimately the students themselves determine how much is learned.

Reinforcement Theories.   Reinforcement is a major determinant in selecting, shaping, maintaining, and eliminating behavior patterns. Reinforcement theory assumes that each reinforcement adds an increment of strength to the desired response. Thus, a sequence of reinforcement will raise the probability that the correct response will occur in a given situation. Learning, one school of thought holds, is shaped by a series of positive rewards that are sequenced to move responses from a generalized direction to very specific acts that are predetermined by the person applying the reinforcement. In the early stages of behavior development, the teacher reinforces rough approximations to the desired response. Later, accurate responses are reinforced, thus influencing the desired pattern of behavior. For example, when you learned to tie your shoes, the first effort was probably fairly tangled. But someone nevertheless congratulated you on a job well done and pointed out how to improve your knot. As you got better, the praise was initially more enthusiastic, and then as you became proficient and the task became routine, the praise tapered off to nothing.

Reinforcement can be provided by an outside force such as the teacher, or by the individual doing the learning. Self-imposed reinforcement is sometimes referred to as *intrinsic reinforcement* and is generally considered to be more effective than external forces in reinforcing behavior on a long-term basis. There are several extensions of the basic idea of using reinforcement to shape desired behavior. One such reinforcement theory is based on a multifactor approach and explains learning as the product of a combination of conditions that are necessary for learning. These conditions are motivation, cues, responses, and reward. *Motivation* stems from basic human needs, such as hunger, and continues to more social needs, such as the need for approval; and on to the desire to understand and to solve problems. This type of motivation will direct the learner toward goal-directed behavior. *Cues* are those stimuli perceived by the learner that determine the type and timing of action that is to be made. *Responses* are those overt and covert attempts made by the learner to solve the problem. *Rewards* (reinforcement) are given for those responses that represent the behavior to be strengthened. The reinforcement, in addition to rewarding the behavior, provides information that allows the learner to improve performance and to master concepts. Information returned to the learner in this manner is referred to as *feedback*. Feedback is essential to the improvement of skills and the retention of knowledge. Some theorists regard this information/ feedback aspect of reinforcement as being the most important.

In applying reinforcement theory, the teacher first must determine the components of complex concepts and skills to be taught and arrange them in a hierarchical order. (This is done in task analysis, which is explained and discussed in Chapter 5.) Instruction should aim at cuing students and initiating behavior that students are expected to perform. Feedback and reward should be provided immediately after performance. However, reward is most effective in terms of ensuring desired behavior if it is provided intermittently.

Numerous principles, or laws, of learning have evolved from the theories discussed in this section. These are the things that we know for sure about how people learn. Some of these principles and examples of their uses are found in the next section.

Principles of Learning

Certain conditions, or principles, under which learning takes place have been identified through years of practice and much research. The teacher of occupational subjects should have a near-expert grasp of these principles and their application to the act of teaching, since they are vital to the planning, design, and execution of instruction and instructional materials.

The presentation of material is only a part of a teacher's job. Careful planning and preparation *in addition to* a skilled presentation are keys to successful teaching. When preparing new lessons, revising old ones, and designing instructional materials, teachers must always incorporate the principles of learning in order to create teaching and instructional materials that are understandable, learnable, and retainable. A number of principles of learning are explained in the following paragraphs with suggestions as to how they may be applied to teaching (these principles will be referred to again in Chapters 4 and 5).

Learning Is a Process

Learning is an active and continuous process. We can see that learning is occurring or has taken place by changes in behavior and demonstrated growth of knowledge. There are entire college courses and programs devoted to the learning process, so a complete discussion is not possible here. Figure 3.1 is a simplified representation of how the learning process might appear on paper.

In the first step, the motivated learner expects to learn something—their mind is "open" to learning. Then in the second step, as something is taught to them or they read, see, or hear, or otherwise experience something, they apprehend the information and selectively perceive it. The teacher's role in this step is to direct the students' attention to the appropriate aspect of the lesson being taught. It is important to note that not everything that goes in necessarily stays in.

The third step, called acquisition, involves the learner's mind encoding the information in a fashion that will allow for easy retrieval later. You will see later that individuals learn in different ways, so this step is crucial for teachers to be aware of and plan for in their instruction. Teachers help in this step of the process by assisting students to recall relevant materials and planning lessons in such a fashion that will facilitate the storage of information. Step 4 in the learning process is the brain's mechanism for storing information—the way and the where things are tucked away in the recesses. Scientists believe that chemical and electrical components of the brain comprise this step. Teachers usually have no role in the retention phase.

The next logical step in the process is retrieving or recalling what was put in. When the learner is required to use some bit of information, the mind is triggered to recall the information or data and the learner will remember it and retrieve it. Think for a moment of how you remember names or telephone numbers and this process will become more clear. Even though the mind has brought forth the information, learning has still not occurred until the remaining steps have been

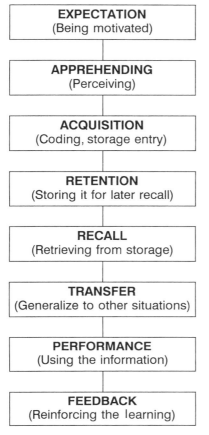

Figure 3.1 The Learning Process

completed. Step 6 in the process is generalizing the data or information that has been retrieved to some other situation. You will recall from the previous section that this is called transfer of learning. Finally, to complete the process, learners have to perform using the information or data in those other, transferred situations, and receive feedback, either through self-evaluation or from an instructor. As you can see, learning involves much more than having information funneled into one's head.

Because this process is a continuous one, students learn even when a teacher is doing a poor job. Unfortunately, most of the learning that takes place in such a situation has a negative tone. Most adults will more readily remember a poor teacher they had in adolescence than they will an average or good teacher. An important point to remember when teaching is the active and continuous nature of learning. Teachers should repeatedly check on student learning through the use of quizzes, tests, oral questions, and classroom observation of skill development.

Styles and Rates of Learning Vary

Learning styles and rates vary from one student to the next. For example, some students learn better by reading than they do by listening; some learn faster than others (even among those who learn best using the same style). It is not uncommon to have learners of five or six types in a single classroom. It is the teacher's job to determine the students' different learning styles and to develop teaching strategies that will best help students to realize their potential.

A detailed examination of learning and teaching styles is beyond the scope of this guide, but a few of the more common styles are briefly described in the following paragraphs. The reader is urged to consult the references found at the end of this chapter for more specific explanations.

Sensory Learners. These students rely on one or more sense for the meaningful formation of ideas. The *sensory specialist* relies primarily on one sense, such as the visual, while the *sensory generalist* uses all or many of the senses to gather information and gain insight. Very few teachers have the luxury or the time to design instructional materials for or adapt teaching styles to each learner, so it is important to incorporate as many of the senses into each learning experience as possible.

Intuitive Learners.   Intuitive learners are able to take advantage of sudden insights, unexplained leaps in thought, and generalizations to master concepts and ideas. Their learning process does not follow what is considered "traditional" logic, or any step-by-step sequence. Intuitive learners tend to work faster than others and to make more wild guesses, but often in the process they lose or do not grasp the evidence that led them to the answer. Teachers can best help intuitive learners by assisting them, through questioning, to retrace their thinking and to specify the evidence that they used to reach a conclusion.

Incremental Learners.   For a long time it was thought that all people learned best in a step-by-step fashion, systematically adding information, like the pieces of a puzzle, to gain a larger understandings. Many people do learn this way, and it is a good practice in teaching to start with small, simple steps and proceed to larger, more complex operations. Remember how you learned arithmetic, progressing from simple to more complex addition on through subtraction and higher mathematics? A common error that occupational teachers make is to assume that, because they, the teacher, are experts in their subject matter and that because they are able to do it, their students will become experts in one quantum leap.

The Principle of Readiness

Students learn dependent upon their readiness to do so, their emotional state, their abilities, and their potential. This principle is related to motivation, and it includes, probably most importantly, the desire to learn.

Individuals learn best when they are ready to learn, and they do not learn much if they see no reason for learning. Getting students ready to learn is usually the teacher's responsibility. If students have a strong purpose, a clear objective, and a well-fixed reason for learning something, they make more progress than if they lack motivation. Readiness implies a degree of single-mindedness and eagerness. When students are ready to learn, they meet the teacher at least halfway, which simplifies the job considerably. Teachers can help enhance this desire by emphasizing the meaningfulness of the subject, exhibiting a sincere enthusiasm for the subject, and by providing incentive to learn.

Another way to get students ready to learn is to provide them with the opportunity to succeed, and to do so as early as possible. This can be done by having the students produce a simple usable or *fun* device or leading them through the solution of a common problem. Success is very satisfying for any student. Therefore, learning takes place more effectively when satisfaction is derived.

The cliché that enthusiasm is contagious is very true in the classroom. The apathetic teacher will undoubtedly have apathetic students. Enthusiasm cannot be artificially created, so the best advice might be, "If you don't have it, don't teach."

Under certain circumstances, the teacher can do little, if anything, to inspire in students a readiness to learn. If outside responsibilities, interests, or worries weigh too heavily on their minds, if their schedules are overcrowded, or if their personal problems seem insoluble, students may have little interest in learning.

Life Experiences

Learning is influenced by the life experiences of the learner. Imagine trying to teach someone how to tie different knots by referring to tying a shoelace. If the student had never tied a shoelace, the reference would be useless. Most teachers will not encounter such extremes, but the point is that we should have some knowledge of the students' backgrounds and past experiences. Helping students to recognize the similarities and differences between past experiences and present situations will smooth the transfer of learning from one situation to the next. In addition, relating what is being learned to what is already known will make the knowledge more personal, or relevant to the student.

Application

Learning is more effective when there is immediate application of what is being taught. Students should be active in terms of thinking, writing, discussion, or problem solving as soon as possible after information is presented. No lesson is complete without application of learned material. Whenever appropriate, the teacher should plan "doing" activities such as practical exercises, return demonstrations, case studies, or group discussions. You will recall from previous paragraphs that this application of knowledge facilitates both the retention of skills or knowledge and its reinforcement.

Knowledge of Progress

Another principle is that learning is facilitated when the learners have knowledge of their progress toward a goal. (Chapter 5 contains a discussion of goals and objectives.) Application of this principle serves two important functions: (1) It prevents students from running down blind alleys, and (2) What they have learned is reinforced by knowledge of success. Determining the degree of progress toward a goal does not always mean testing students, but it's not a bad place to start. Testing can consist of daily quizzes over material covered or observation of performance using a checklist. The tests, quizzes, or observations should be designed to determine what the students know—not what they don't know. And the results should be shared with the students as soon as possible.

Another related principle of learning is that learning is influenced by the learners' perception of themselves and the situation they are in. Everything the teacher can do to help the students succeed will enhance their self-image and make them more comfortable in learning. Each positive experience builds on the last, creating an ever-expanding universe.

Repetition

Practice makes perfect conveys the main idea behind the principle of repetition. In order for learning to take place, the teacher should provide a sufficient number of exposures to the subject material. Each point made during a class should be summarized before proceeding to the next. Students should be allowed multiple opportunities to practice their newly learned skills. Stated in another way, this principle states that those things often repeated are best remembered. It is the reason that we have students practice and drill in order to learn new skills and acquire new knowledge.

The human memory is not infallible. The mind can rarely retain, evaluate, and apply new concepts or practices after only one exposure. Students learn by applying and re-applying what they have been told and shown. Every time practice occurs, learning continues and is reinforced. The teacher must provide opportunities for students to practice or repeat, and they must see that this process is directed toward a goal. Remember, if a concept or skill is important enough to teach, the students will surely need some practice in order to master it.

The Principle of Effect

This principle states that learning is strengthened when accompanied by a pleasant or satisfying feeling, and that learning is weakened when associated with an unpleasant feeling. An experience that produces feelings of defeat, frustration, anger, confusion, or futility are unpleasant for the student. If, for example, a teacher attempts to teach a complicated procedure during the first class, the student is likely to feel inferior and be dissatisfied.

Teachers should be cautious. Impressing students with the difficulty of a problem, a technique, or a job duty can make the teaching task difficult. Usually it is better to tell students that a problem or task, although difficult, is within their capacity to understand or perform. Whatever the learning situation, it should contain elements that affect the students positively and give them a feeling of satisfaction.

Primacy

Primacy, the state of being first, often creates a strong, almost unshakable, impression. For the teacher, this means that what is taught must be taught right the first time. For the student, it means that learning must be right the first time. "Unlearning" and "unteaching" are much more difficult than learning and teaching done correctly the first time. If, for example, a student learns a faulty technique, the task of teaching the correct technique will be more difficult because the student will already have a strong sense of the way to do it, even though that way is incorrect. Every student's learning process should be started correctly. The first experience should be positive and functional and lay the foundation for all that is to follow.

Intensity

A vivid, dramatic, or exciting learning experience teaches more than a routine or boring experience. A student is likely to gain greater understanding of job skills by performing them than from merely reading about them. The principle of intensity, then, suggests that a student will learn more from the real thing than from a substitute. The classroom does impose limitations on the amount of realism that can be brought into teaching. The teacher should use imagination in approaching reality as closely as possible. Mockups, colored slides, films, filmstrips, charts, posters, photographs, and other audiovisual aids can add vividness to classroom instruction.

Recency

This principle states that the things most recently learned are the best remembered. Conversely, the further a student is removed in time from a new fact or understanding, the more difficult it is to remember it. It is easy, for example, for a student to recall a number used a few minutes earlier, but it is usually impossible to remember an unfamiliar one used a week earlier. Teachers recognize the principle of recency when they carefully plan a summary for a lesson, a laboratory period, or a post-lesson critique. The teacher repeats, re-states, or re-emphasizes important points at the end of a lesson to make sure that the student remembers them. The principle of recency often determines the relative positions of lectures within a course of instruction.

Levels of Learning

Since the 1950s educators have classified learning into several *domains* and further into levels within those domains. The three most common domains are the *cognitive*, the *affective*, and the *psychomotor*. The cognitive domain is concerned with knowledge such as facts and figures. The affective domain includes the development of attitudes and feelings, while the psychomotor domain is concerned with the development of motor skills. Experts in the psychology of learning have divided each of the three domains into levels of learning; six for the cognitive domain, five for the affective, and four for the psychomotor.

For our purposes, a three-level classification system (applicable to each domain) is adequate and appropriate to the majority of learned activities within occupational education. These levels are determined by careful study of the tasks of the occupation being taught. An occupational analysis (see Chapter 5) will help determine the degree of manipulative skill needed, the technical knowledge required, the frequency with which specific tasks are performed, the hazards inherent in the tasks, and the extent to which specialization is required.

Level 1–General Knowledge

In the three-level classification of learning, the first level is concerned primarily with the students' ability to follow directions. In order to perform most jobs, it is necessary to remember facts, so instruction is given to such a depth that students will recognize an item after their memory is jogged. This level, general knowledge, requires sufficient knowledge of relationships and associated principles needed in order to make information being learned meaningful. Students should know sources from which they might obtain information, and they must develop the ability to follow directions. This level of learning generally requires no manipulation of instruments other than pencils, and few, if any, practical hands-on exercises are used during instructional activities. Instructional activities that will achieve a general knowledge include lecture, supervised research, reading assignments, or some paper and pencil problem solving.

General knowledge is characterized by:

1. Remembering facts
2. Recognizing items in response to prompts
3. Matching items to establish relationships
4. Classifying ideas and generalizations
5. Following written and oral directions

Level 2–Working Knowledge

The second level of learning, working knowledge, concerns the depth to which a student successfully recalls something that has been learned previously. The students' abilities are developed to the degree that they can interpret diagrams, drawings, tables, and information in manuals. At this level, the students develop abilities to do such things as translate verbal or written statements (word problems) into symbolic statements, and vice versa. Manipulative skills are usually performed at a limited level and are developed to perform basic operations. Working knowledge is characterized by:

1. Recalling specific information
2. Interpreting diagrams, drawings, tables, symbols, and graphs
3. Translating mathematical statements and verbal or written statements back and forth
4. Performance of basic manipulative skills *with* supervision

The development of a working knowledge of an occupation can be readily achieved by means of conferences, demonstrations, lead-through exercises, and supervised practice.

Level 3–Qualified Knowledge

The top level in the three-level classification system is termed qualified knowledge. This level denotes the process by which a student, faced with a new problem or situation, has the ability to recognize common factors and bring new sources and types of information to bear on a new solution. At this level, knowledge and skills are learned in sufficient breadth and depth for the student to transfer earlier learnings to a new set of circumstances, including reflecting on the consequences expected if an action is taken. Manipulative skills are developed whereby performance of a task is efficiently and smoothly executed. Qualified knowledge is characterized by these abilities.

1. Recognizing common factors that apply to a new problem or situation.
2. Transferring earlier learnings to the solution of new situations.

3. The ability to analyze or synthesize in order to maintain continual operation of an intricate system and its components.
4. Weighing the consequences resulting from any action taken.
5. Planning and performing all specified task-oriented manipulations with a high degree of skill and *without supervision.*

To obtain the level of qualified knowledge, instruction should be geared to develop the students' abilities to apply principles, concepts, and theories to new situations. Level 3 provides a base for transfer of learning, so that when students are employed they can perform productively with a minimum of additional job training or supervision. To accomplish this level of learning requires the inclusion of extensive practical exercises in the instructional program.

It is usually not necessary to learn all things to the highest level in a classroom situation. To attempt to teach all parts of a course to Level 3 would be both unrealistic and too time-consuming, even if it was possible. Electronics technicians must know something about the characteristics and kinds of solder (Level 1), and they must actually solder connections using manufacturer's specifications (Level 2); but they do not need the transfer knowledge about solder that might be needed by a metallurgist or a research worker for a manufacturer of solder. On the other hand, their ability to analyze and trace circuits must be transferable to devices that they have never seen (Level 3).

Each instructional activity is classified at the highest level to which the students have to learn or perform it in order to be successful on the job. Precisely stating the level of learning required will assist teachers in determining what the students will do, the conditions under which it will be done, and the level of minimum acceptable performance.

Individual Differences

The section of this chapter on principles of learning contained some discussion on individual styles of learning. This section contains a discussion of other individual differences that can affect our teaching and the way the students learn.

Age

The art or science of teaching is called pedagogy. The word means "study of (or about) children" from the Greek *paed*, or child. Until recently, research in education and the psychology of learning was limited to how children or nonhumans, such as monkeys, learned. Researchers such as Jean Piaget and Lawrence Kohlberg (see references) have determined that children pass through phases and stages of development. The conditions for teaching and learning change by phase or stage. Children at different ages are motivated by different things and learn in different fashions. Most of this research has been concentrated on the early years of life, birth to about age 18.

Like children, adults too, pass through developmental stages. This means that adults' needs and interests change as they age and that values continue to grow and change. As the age of the typical occupational education student continues to rise, knowledge of adult developmental stages becomes increasingly more important for teachers.

Some of the differences between how adults and children learn follow. Remember, these differences are general; that is, they do not always apply. (For more specific examples, see the references listed at the end of the chapter.)

Direction. Adults often prefer self-directed and self-designed learning activities over group learning experiences led by a teacher. Children prefer the opposite, especially until they gain sufficient skill and confidence to work on their own. This does not mean that adults can or should be left to fend for themselves in the classroom. It does mean that adult learners should be included in the planning of how they will go about learning the task or information at hand.

Ego Involvement. Adults in the classroom generally have more to lose in terms of ego and self-esteem than children. Many adults have had bad experiences with education and are more reluctant than children are to risk trying new behavior in front of peers. It is safe to assume that adults are more preoccupied with worldly events that affect them personally outside of the classroom than are children.

Life Experiences. By virtue of the fact that adults have "been around," they bring life experiences to the classroom that children cannot. These life experiences, depending on how successful they were, can have profound effects on the way people learn and the time it takes them to do it. Teachers will do well to learn at the outset of instruction what the experiences of their students are in relation to the subject. In order to teach students what they should know, it is necessary to know what they already know.

Expectations. Adults have expectations about what they want to learn. Children usually do not develop such sophisticated thought processes until well into the teenage years. It is critical, when teaching adults, to very carefully clarify and articulate all expectations before getting into content. Expectations should be clarified with children, too, but it is more crucial with adults.

Keep in mind that all people, whether they are children or adults, are *individuals*—they are all different. Children, adults, and adolescents all mature at different rates and to different degrees.

Intelligence

Learners also differ in intelligence. Recent years have seen quite a controversy among educators, psychologists, lawyers, and others over the issue of intelligence. One of the most recent writers and researchers on intelligence is Howard Gardner who believes that there are at least seven separate human capacities that range from musical or artistic intelligence to the type of intelligence involved in understanding oneself.

For our purposes, intelligence may be defined as the ability to respond rapidly and successfully to new or unusual situations. Intelligence allows the learner to link new experiences and ideas to past experience and stored knowledge. If one believes that there is such a thing as intelligence (whatever its type or definition might be) and that it can be determined and measured, then it is safe to say that some people are more intelligent than others. It would be rare to find a group of students who were all at the same level of intelligence. This fact is of particular significance when designing curriculum materials and learning activities. Materials cannot be geared exclusively to one end or the other of the intelligence continuum but, instead, have to provide a meaningful and challenging learning opportunity for all students. This often requires the development of several sets of materials and the use of a variety of learning activities. Out-of-class assignments are helpful because they allow all students an opportunity to achieve the minimum level of knowledge at an individual, more comfortable pace. Encouraging questions in class is an excellent technique for minimizing individual differences. Some students can clear up misunderstandings and catch up on missed information while others can satisfy curiosity about finer, nice-to-know points. Quite obviously, teachers have to have more than one trick in their bags!

Gender

There is no evidence to show that, because of their gender, males and females learn differently. There *is* evidence to show that because of social and cultural conditioning, males and females sometimes learn differently or have different aptitudes. In other words, if males and females learn differently, it *may* be gender-related, but there is no evidence to show that it is gender-specific. It is important not to stereotype individuals in roles or learning styles. There is a growing body of evidence that shows if we expect someone to do something or act in a specific way, that person will live up (or down) to our expectations. Expect only the best of your students, do it consistently, and they will perform positively.

Level of Concentration

The ability to fix or focus attention on an idea or instruction is called concentration. The power of concentration varies widely among individuals, especially between children and adults. Teachers generally are advised to limit sustained lectures and demonstrations to ten or so minutes at a time. After speaking or demonstrating for ten minutes, the students should be allowed to practice or be given some other activity that will take advantage of the natural break in concentration. This activity should also only be about ten minutes in length and then the lecture or demonstration may be resumed.

Students with Disabilities

A host of federal and state laws mandate equal educational opportunity for individuals with disabilities. Many students in occupational education programs are there to retrain for a new occupation after injury or illness. A few of the conditions that you will encounter in the classroom are briefly described below with some hints on how to provide successful learning experiences.

It is important to remember that some students with disabilities do not view themselves as disabled. For example, persons who have been blind or deaf from birth or infancy learn from the beginning of their lives to cope with the world in a fashion that is different—they do what is necessary for them. A rule to follow for students with disabilities is not to preconceive either ability or inability. Let the individuals themselves decide what they can and cannot do.

The question, Why do disabilities affect learning?, is often asked. The answer depends on the disability, but a few examples may help. Some persons who have physical injuries may be in constant pain as a result of their condition. Others may be taking required medication. Both of the conditions will impact on the student's ability to concentrate on and readily absorb instruction. Other individuals may be very self-conscious and will try to avoid some of the intense interaction necessary in a learning situation. Experience has shown repeatedly that virtually all of the so-called disabilities can be dealt with in the classroom. Like most other endeavors, it merely requires an openness and willingness to try on the part of the teacher and the student.

Some excellent resources for learning about students with disabilities and for teaching them may be found in the references section. (You are encouraged to consult them.)

Students Who Are Deaf or Hard of Hearing.   A student who is deaf has a hearing loss that is so severe that the processing of sounds, with or without amplification, is so limited as to adversely affect ways that the student can learn. Hard of hearing means a hearing impairment that adversely affects the way a student learns but that is not included under the definition of deaf. Students who are deaf or hard of hearing rely more on sight and other senses. Visual aids should be used whenever possible, and procedures and directions should be written out. Interpreters, or signers, are often available to assist. In any case, the students should always have a clear line of sight to the teacher or the demonstration being performed. Many students who are deaf read lips, so it is necessary to always speak facing in their direction.

Students Who Are Blind.   A person is considered to be visually handicapped when they have a visual impairment which, even with correction, adversely affects their educational performance. Visually handicapped people are usually classified as "legally blind" or "partially sighted." The number of competitively employed people who are blind has nearly doubled in recent years, in large part as a result of their increased participation in occupational education programs. Rehabilitation counselors will assist the occupational teacher in adapting curriculum and methods for teaching the blind.

Students Who Are Mentally Disabled.   Students who are mentally disabled may have significant subaverage general intellectual functioning existing concurrently with deficits in adaptive behavior. There are varying degrees and numerous causes of mental disabilities. Occupational education teachers most often encounter mentally disabled people who are classified as mildly or moderately disabled. The mildly or moderately mentally disabled person can be expected to obtain competitive employment and to function in daily community life. Remediation and educational approaches vary with the type and cause of mental disability. Education programs for the mentally disabled are determined from tests of specific skills, actual classroom performance, general health, and conferences with teachers, counselors, and parents.

Orthopedically Disabled.   Generally, an orthopedically impaired person is one who has a physical defect or malfunction that adversely affects their educational performance. The types and causes are too numerous to detail here, but it should be sufficient to say that the orthopedically impaired person, depending on the disability, can usually be taught in the occupational classroom with removal of architectural barriers.

Other Disabilities.   Other impairments that adversely affect educational performance include speech impairments, heart conditions, asthma, epilepsy, diabetes, emotional disturbances, and other specific learning disabilities. There are various approaches used to work with individuals, whatever their handicapping condition. In most instances, before a handicapped individual is placed in or chooses to be in your class, you will be consulted and assisted in the development of activities to best meet their needs.

Students Who Are Disadvantaged

Disadvantaged persons are individuals who because of economic, social, cultural, language, or other conditions have difficulty in succeeding in the regular school environment. Most disadvantaged people have experienced doors closing in their faces, preconceived attitudes of others that are not based on actual evaluation, and nonexistent or elusive job opportunities. Such individuals often lack verbal communication skills and the motivation to learn. Materials used in the instruction of the disadvantaged must have high interest and be written to an ability level that allows immediate success. Most programs for the disadvantaged need to be individualized so that students may proceed along their own path of achievement. Programs for the disadvantaged are effective when the students feel that they have been selected for special consideration and when they feel that the program has helped them be successful at doing something. Teachers of the disadvantaged have to be flexible and adaptive while still providing a program that will ready students for making decisions and performing on the job.

Cultural Differences

The years from the late 1970s to the present have been a period of immigration to the United States that, at least in numbers, has been without precedent. The dominant culture of the United States was shaped by the immigrants who built the country and their ancestors who followed them here. Recent immigration has been largely from Asia and the Middle East. It is important that the teacher understand that culture is what guides us in our thinking, feeling, and acting. Culture is learned and shared by people and it determines what values and behaviors are exhibited. Culture is symbolically represented through language and how people interact. Culture is *not* ethnicity, nor is it race or religion. Culture is not a list of traits, facts, or materials used by a people, nor is culture higher class status that is derived from a knowledge of art, music, literature, or manners.

Persons who enter our classrooms who are from different cultures are struggling to learn through different "filters" than mainstream Americans. Successful teachers become aware of the culture in themselves and the culture in others. By doing this we become aware that the thought processes that occur within each of us also occur within others, but that they may take on a different shape or meaning. Teachers need to remember that there are many cultural ways that are correct.

Summary

An event of learning is a relatively permanent change that can be observed in the behavior of a person. There are four major categories of learning theories—motivation theories, transfer of learning theories, retention theories, and reinforcement theories. The practice of teaching has revealed a number of principles of learning including: it is a process, people have different styles of learning, students learn dependent on their readiness to do so, and learning is more effective when there is immediate application of what is being taught.

Learning has been classified into several domains and can be further classified into levels within those domains. The three levels of learning appropriate to occupational education are general knowledge, working knowledge, and qualified knowledge. To accomplish a level of learning sufficient for entry level in an occupation requires the inclusion of extensive practical exercises in the instructional program.

Learning and teaching are affected by the extensive number of differences people bring to the classroom. Some of these differences include age, level of maturation, intelligence, life experiences, and various disabilities.

For Further Reading

Learning Theories and Principles

DeCecco, J.P. (1970). *The Psychology of Learning and Instruction.* Englewood Cliffs, NJ: Prentice-Hall,

Gagne, R.M. (1970). *The Conditions of Learning.* Second Edition. New York: Holt, Rinehart and Winston.

Gagne, R.M. (1974). *Essentials of Learning for Instruction.* Hinsdale, IL: The Dryden Press.

Maslow, A.H. (1968). *Toward a Psychology of Being.* Second Edition. Princeton, NJ: Van Nostrand.

Maslow, A.H. (1970). *Motivation and Personality.* Second Edition. New York: Harper and Row.

Hilgard, E.R. (Ed.) (1964). *Theories of Learning and Instruction.* Sixty-third Yearbook of the National Society for the Study of Education. Part I. Bloomington, Illinois: Public School Publishing Company.

Learning Styles

Anderson, J., and Adams, M. (1992). "Acknowledging the Learning Styles of Diverse Student Populations." *New Directions for Teaching and Learning* 49: 19–32 (Spring).

Dunn, R.S., and Dunn, K.J. (1979). "Learning Styles/ Teaching Styles: Should They . . . Can They . . . Be Matched?" *Educational Leadership,* January, 237–244.

Fischer, B.B. and Fischer, L. (1979). "Styles in Teaching and Learning." *Educational Leadership,* January, 245–254.

Individual Differences

Banks, J.A. (1981). *Multiethnic Education: Theory and Practice.* Boston: Allyn & Bacon.

Garcia, Ricardo L. (1982). *Teaching in a Pluralistic Society: Concepts, Models, Strategies.* New York: Harper and Row.

Gardner, H. (1993). *Multiple Intelligences: The Theory in Practice.* New York: Basic Books

Gearhart, B.R., and Weishahn, M.W. (1976). *The Handicapped Child in the Regular Classroom.* St. Louis, Missouri: C.V. Mosby Company.

Haslam, R.A., and Valletutti, P.J. (1975). *Medical Problems in the Classroom.* Boston: University Park Press.

Inhelder, B., and Piaget, J. (1964). *The Early Growth of Logic in the Child.* New York: Harper and Row.

Kidd, J.R. (1959). *How Adults Learn.* New York: Association Press.

Knowles, M.S. (1970). *The Modern Practice of Adult Education.* New York: Association Press.

Piaget, J. (1952). *The Origins of Intelligence in Children.* New York: International Universities Press.

Pitton, D, Warring, D., Frank, K., and Hunter, S. (1993). *Multicultural Messages: Nonverbal Communication in the Classroom.* (ERIC Document Reproduction Service Number ED 362 519)

Reece, B.L. (1978). *Teaching Adults: A Guide for Vocational Instructors.* Arlington, Virginia: American Vocational Association.

Schorr, L. (1989). *Within Our Reach: Breaking the Cycle of Disadvantage.* New York: Doubleday.

Sheehy, G. (1977). *Passages: Predictable Crises of Adult Life.* New York: Dutton.

Slavin, R.E., and Madden, N.A. (1989, February). "What Works for Students at Risk: A Research Synthesis." *Educational Leadership* 46: 4–13.

Schmeck, R.R. (Ed.) (1988). *Learning Strategies and Learning Styles.* New York: Plenum Press.

Smith, R.M. et al. (1990). *Learning to Learn Across the Life Span.* San Francisco: Jossey–Bass.

Wallin, D. (1996). "Multicultural Education and the Vocational/Technical Student." *Community College Journal of Research and Practice* 20: 23–33 (January-February).

Walker, J.T. (1996). *The Psychology of Learning: Principles and Processes.* Upper Saddle River, NJ: Prentice-Hall.

Discussion Questions

1. Define learning and give an example from your occupational area.

   _____

   _____

   _____

2. What is the purpose of having or studying theories of how people learn?

   _____

   _____

   _____

3. How are the senses used in the learning process? What senses could you appeal to in teaching your occupation?

   _____

   _____

   _____

4. How do individual differences among students affect learning in a classroom? What consequences does this have for the teacher?

   _____

   _____

   _____

5. What is a learning style? Give a concrete example of several learning styles.

   _____

   _____

   _____

6. Explain what "level of learning" is. Give an example from your occupation for each of the three levels described in this chapter.

   _____

   _____

Exercises

1. Give an example of a "behavior" practiced in your classroom that would be appropriate for the definition of learning described in this chapter.

   _____

   _____

2. Give an example of change in behavior that would _not_ be classified as learning as it is described in this chapter.

   _____

   _____

3. Give one example of how each of the senses could be used in an instructional situation for your occupation.

   Sight: _____

   Hearing: _____

   Touch: _____

   Smell: _____

   Taste: _____

4. Given the phases in the learning process, choose a skill or bit of knowledge from your occupation and describe how in the teaching process you might anticipate and enhance the process or concept. For example, if you are teaching background information about your subject (principles), how would you motivate the students? How would you assist them in comprehending the subject? How much practice should you provide to enhance retention?

   a. Motivation   _____

   b. Apprehending   _____

   c. Acquisition   _____

   d. Retention   _____

   e. Recall   _____

   f. Generalization _____

   g. Performance   _____

   h. Feedback   _____

5. Review the principles of learning described in this chapter and give an instructional situation (from teaching your occupation) for eight of the principles.

    a. _____

    b. _____

    c. _____

    d. _____

    e. _____

    f. _____

    g. _____

    h. _____

6. List at least three ways in which individuals differ as discussed in this chapter.

    a. _____

    b. _____

    c. _____

    d. _____

7. List one method a teacher could use to compensate in the classroom for each of those individual differences listed in exercise 6.

    a. _____

    b. _____

    c. _____

    d. _____

4 What? Me a Teacher?

Assuming the Role of a Teacher

YOUR STUDENTS WILL HAVE a variety of needs, and in assuming the role of a teacher, you will need to be aware of those needs. In this chapter we will examine those needs, present pointers on how you can meet those needs, and discuss how you can establish and control the environment in which those needs will be met so that learning will take place. Finally, some traits of successful teachers are examined.

Successful teachers have a solid, healthy, and productive relationship with students. Most of the credit for this success goes to the teacher's knowledge of students as human beings and of the needs, drives, and desires they continually try to satisfy in one way or another. As we discuss these needs, notice that these needs are human needs—they apply to all. The needs described are arranged in a hierarchical order first suggested and elaborated on by the late Abraham Maslow, a psychologist from Brandeis University.

Student Needs

Dr. Maslow placed human needs in the shape of a pyramid with basic needs such as food, rest, and protection from the elements, at the pyramid's base. The existence of these needs, termed *physical needs*, prevent learning or self-expression until they are met. Once the needs are satisfied, they no longer provide motivation, so individuals strive to satisfy the needs of the next higher level in the pyramid—safety needs.

The *safety needs* include protection against danger, threat, and deprivation. Some educators and psychologists call safety needs "security needs." Whatever the label, the needs are real, and student behavior is affected by them. The theory holds that if individuals are physically comfortable and have no fear for their safety, the next level of needs will become the prime influence on their behavior.

The third level of needs, *social needs*, includes the need to belong, to associate with others, and to give and receive friendship and love. The classroom is not a "normal" environment for most people, so it becomes easier to understand that their need for association and for belonging during instruction will often be more pronounced and may be manifested in their behavior.

Maslow called the fourth level of needs the *egoistic needs*. These needs will usually have a very direct influence on the student-teacher relationship. Egoistic needs are of two kinds: (1) those that relate to self-esteem—needs for self-confidence, for independence, for achievement, for competence, for knowledge; and (2) those that relate to reputation—needs for status, for recognition, for appreciation, and for the deserved respect of peers. The ability to recognize egoistic needs and help students meet them is one of the most crucial assets of a good teacher.

At the apex of the pyramid of human needs are those for *self-fulfillment*, for realizing individual potentialities, for continued development, and for being creative in the broadest sense of that term. Aiding students to achieve self-fulfillment is perhaps the most worthwhile accomplishment of a teacher.

It should be noted that occupational education equips people to meet all of their needs. By teaching people job skills, we provide them with the means to satisfy their physical and safety needs. Work skills well-learned will lead to productivity in the workplace, which is itself a society. Working takes up at least a third of our time, and over half of our waking time. Thus, work and the workplace are probably the dominant factors in most people's lives. Occupational education and work play major roles in helping people meet their social and egoistic needs. Maslow postulated that happy, self-confident people who are respected by their peers will be those who are self-fulfilled.

A Climate for Learning

Teachers should strive to help the students satisfy their needs in a manner that will ensure a healthful environment for learning, and there are several rules (or principles, if you will) of *teaching* that will foster a healthful climate. Following these seven rules will minimize student frustrations and help achieve good human relations in the classroom.

Keep Students Motivated

Students gain much more from wanting to learn than from being forced to learn. All too often students do not realize how a particular lesson or course can help them reach an important goal. When they see the benefits or purposes of a lesson or course, their enjoyment and their efforts will increase. Have you ever been forced to learn or memorize something? Did you enjoy it? Can you now remember anything but the experience? (This point will be discussed further in Chapter 5.) Teachers can maintain a high level of motivation in the students by varying their methods of instruction, by continually providing examples from the workplace that are relevant to the students' experiences, and judiciously following the remaining six rules as they teach.

Keep Students Informed

Students feel insecure when they do not know what is expected of them or what is going to happen to them. Teachers can minimize such feelings of insecurity by telling students what is expected of them and what they can expect from the teacher and the learning experience. This can be done in various ways, such as by giving them an overview of the course; specifying performance objectives; keeping them posted on their progress; and by giving them adequate notice of examinations, assignments, or other requirements. It is a good practice to tell the students each day what they will be doing in class and what they can expect to learn. Many teachers will begin each lesson with a phrase that goes something like "Today we will spend our time on the topic of . . . , When you leave class today you should be able to . . . , or you will know . . .". An often overlooked aspect of keeping students informed is to provide them with immediate (or as close to immediate as possible) feedback on homework and examinations. This is especially important if the homework or answers on the examination were incorrect. The longer the student is left wondering or assuming that what they did was correct, the harder it is to re-learn the material correctly.

Approach Students as Individuals

When teachers limit their thinking to the whole group without considering the individuals who make up that group, their effort is directed at an average personality that really fits no one person. Each group has its own personality that stems from the characteristics and interactions of its members. However, each person within the group has a personality that is unique and should be constantly considered. Remember what was covered in the last chapter about individual differences.

Give Credit When Due

When students do something extremely well, they wish their abilities and efforts to be noticed or they will become frustrated. Praise or credit from the teacher is usually ample reward and provides an incentive to do even better. When praise is deserved, it pays dividends in student effort and achievement. Praise given too freely however, becomes valueless. This rule is related to keeping students informed. As you make your way around the room while students are practicing or working, it is always appropriate to acknowledge the students' progress with a simple statement such as "Good work," or "That's right, keep at it." Practicing this technique will let the students know that you are paying attention to what they are doing and that they are doing it right.

Criticize Positively

Although it is important to give praise and credit when deserved, it is equally important to identify mistakes and failures. To tell students that they have made errors and not provide explanations does not help them. If a student who has made an earnest effort is told that the work is not satisfactory with no other explanation, that student will become frustrated. How many times have you received a paper or assignment back and have been given 17.5 out of 20 possible points and not found a correction on the paper? Errors cannot be corrected if they are not identified; and if they are not identified, they will probably be perpetuated through faulty practice. If, however, the student is briefed on the errors made and is told how to correct them, progress and accomplishment can be made.

Be Consistent

Students want to please their teacher. This is the same desire that influences much of the behavior of subordinates toward their employers in industry and business. Naturally, students have a keen interest in knowing what is required to please the teacher. If the same thing is acceptable one day and not acceptable the next, the student becomes confused. The teacher's philosophy and actions must, therefore, be consistent.

Admit Errors

No one, including the students, expects a teacher to be perfect. The teacher can win the respect of students by honestly acknowledging mistakes. If the teacher tries to cover up or bluff, the students will be quick to sense it. Such behavior tends to destroy student confidence. If in doubt about some point, admit it to the students, but then get the answer and relate it to them as soon as possible.

These seven practices for maintaining a healthful climate are but a few of the many attitudes that can help students learn. (Look ahead to the next chapter to see how they are derived from and relate to the principles of learning that are described there.)

Traits of the Teacher

Your teacher colleagues come in all sizes, shapes, and manners of dress. Which of them are successful? Why? Most teachers, especially of occupational subjects, are not chosen to be teachers because they *already are* good teachers. They are usually chosen because they have demonstrated something that would indicate they *could become* good teachers. They have the required amount of formal education, they have the ability, the discipline, and the character that good teachers must have. Even with all these qualities, good teachers are not just born. Your colleagues who are good teachers evolved by a long and continuous process of education and experience in the classroom. Teachers are in the position to help others develop new skills, to do their jobs better, to learn how to learn, and to acquire and live by the ideals that make society productive.

You will recall from Chapter 1 that teaching an occupation is a second career—one that is in addition to actually practicing the occupation. Occupational teachers are the key persons who transmit the knowledge and skills from one generation of employees to the next. It is clear that teachers must be true professionals. Teachers of occupational subjects must be fully qualified in their occupation, but their ability must go far beyond this if the requirements of professionalism are to be met. Although no single definition can encompass all of the qualifications and considerations of professionalism, the following might be included:

1. Professionalism exists only when a service is performed for someone or for the common good.
2. Professionalism is achieved only after extended training and preparation.
3. True performance as a professional is based on study and research.
4. Professionalism presupposes an intellectual requirement. Professionals must be able to reason logically and accurately.
5. Professionalism requires the ability to make good judgmental decisions. Professionals cannot limit their actions and decisions to standard patterns and practice.

6. Professionalism demands a code of ethics. Professionals must be true to themselves and the ideals of their occupation and to those they serve. Anything less than a sincere performance is quickly detected and immediately destroys their effectiveness.

To try to teach occupational subjects without any one of these qualities can only result in poor performance and poorly prepared students.

Professionalism also includes the teacher's public image. Lately, teachers, all too often, have been willing to accept a less-than-professional status in the public view by relaxing their demeanor, appearance, and approach to their profession. A teacher who gives the impression that interest in teaching is secondary to interest in other activities cannot retain the reputation of a professional. This does not mean that the part-time teacher cannot be a professional, but it does mean that during the time devoted to teaching this individual should present a professional public image.

The professional educator earns the respect of associates; deserves and receives higher pay; and, most importantly, delivers more effective instruction. Some of the basic traits of a professional teacher are discussed in the following sections.

Sincerity

The professional teacher is straightforward and honest. Attempting to hide some inadequacy behind a smokescreen of unrelated instruction will make it impossible to command the interest and attention of the students.

Teaching is predicated upon the students' acceptance of the teacher as a competent, qualified teacher and an expert in the subject matter. Pretentiousness, whether it is real or mistakenly inferred by the student, will immediately cause a loss of confidence by the student in the teacher, and little learning will be accomplished.

The effectiveness of what is taught—for example, emphasis on the precepts of safety—will be lost if the teacher appears to disregard them; the same applies to the teacher's insistence on precision and accuracy in the handling of tools, instruments, materials, and equipment. The professional teacher is honest in every way.

Acceptance of the Student

The professional teacher accepts students as they are, with all their faults and all their problems. The student is a person who wants to learn, and the teacher is a person who is available to help in the learning process. Beginning with this understanding, the professional relationship of the teacher with the student should be based on a mutual acknowledgment that both the student and the teacher are important to each other and that both are working toward the same objective.

Under no circumstance does the professional teacher do anything that degrades the student. Acceptance, rather than ridicule, and support, rather than reproof, will encourage learning, regardless of whether the student is quick to learn or is slow and apprehensive. Criticizing a student who does not learn rapidly is not unlike a physician reprimanding a patient who does not get well as rapidly as was hoped.

Personal Appearance and Habits

Personal appearance has an important effect on the professional image of the teacher. This does not mean that teachers should assume an attire foreign to the actual employment environment or one that would prove unsafe. However, since the teacher is engaged in a learning situation and is interacting with persons other than those found in the workplace, the clothing worn should be appropriate to a professional status. It helps to remember that teachers of occupational subjects actually have to remain committed to two careers: their occupation and teaching. Think of the good teachers you have had. How did they dress?

Personal habits have a significant effect on the professional image. The exercise of common courtesy is perhaps the most important of these. A teacher who is rude, thoughtless, and inattentive cannot earn the respect of students, regardless of technical ability.

Cleanliness of body, breath, and clothing is important to instruction. Most teaching occurs inside, in close proximity to students, so even little annoyances may provide serious distractions from the learning tasks at hand.

Demeanor

The attitude and movements of the teacher can contribute much to a professional image. The good teacher avoids erratic movements, distracting speech habits, and capricious changes in mood. The professional image requires and effective instruction is fostered by the development of a calm, thoughtful, and disciplined, but not somber, demeanor. A forbidding or imperious demeanor is as much to be avoided as is an air of flippancy. The teacher should maintain a personal image of competence and genuine interest in the student's learning tasks.

Safety Practices and Accident Prevention

The safety habits of the teacher, both during instruction and as observed by students when conducting demonstrations or when working in the classroom, have a vital effect on safety. Students consider their teacher to be a paragon of proficiency whose habits they, consciously or unconsciously, attempt to imitate. Advocacy and description of safety practices mean little to a student if the teacher is observed to violate them.

For this reason, teachers must meticulously observe the safety practices taught the students. Habitual observance of regulations, safety precautions, and the precepts of courtesy will enhance the teacher's image of professionalism. More importantly, such habits make the teacher more effective by developing the same habits in the students.

Proper and Correct Language

The professional teacher avoids the use of profanity and obscene language. The professional teacher also uses the English language correctly. The use of profanity or poor English leads to distrust or, at best, to a lack of complete confidence by the students. To many people, such language is actually objectionable to the point of being painful. The professional teacher must speak normally, without inhibitions, positively, and descriptively without resorting to excesses of language.

Beginning occupational education students are entering a realm of new concepts and experiences and are encountering new terms and phrases that are often confusing. Teachers do, and properly should, use terms and phrases unique to an occupation during instruction. However, it is important to carefully define new phrases and terms at the point of instruction when they occur. Do not assume that all students understand all terms and acronyms that are common to an occupation.

The professional teacher uses correct English in all oral and written communications with students. Nothing is more inconsistent than a teacher who demands excellence from students, yet uses incorrect grammar or misspells or incorrectly punctuates written instructional materials. Virtually every computer word processing program contains a spelling checker and most have provisions for grammar checking. Make it a habit to not exit the program without first executing those routines. Then, proofread all materials before printing them for distribution to students.

Self-Improvement

Professional teachers never become complacent or satisfied with their own qualifications and abilities. They are constantly active and alert for ways to improve their qualifications, effectiveness, and the services they provide to students.

There are many opportunities for self-improvement available to teachers of occupational subjects. Many companies sponsor seminars on new equipment and materials. Universities offer inservice training clinics or workshops, which are valuable sources of new techniques and refresher training while also offering opportunities to exchange information with teachers from other areas. Local and state departments of education usually have funds that are set aside specifically for inservice training workshops of all kinds.

Professional journals, subject matter periodicals, government publications, and technical issuances from business or industry are other sources of valuable information for teachers. In addition to journals and government publications, a number of excellent handbooks and other reference materials are available from commercial publishers. Also, most public and university libraries have excellent resource material on educational psychology, teaching methods, testing, and technical subjects. Professional teachers have the ability to knowledgeably read research, and they actively seek the latest research in both their occupational area and in teaching as sources for adding to their teaching repertoire.

Adequate Instruction

The professional teacher attempts to carefully and correctly analyze the personality, the thinking, the needs, and the ability of each student. Since no two students are alike, the same methods of instruction cannot be equally effective for all students. This analysis requires that the teacher talk to students at some length to learn about the individual's background, interests, way of thinking, and temperament. A teacher who has not correctly analyzed a student may soon find that the instruction is not producing the desired results.

The demands on teachers to serve as practical psychologists are much greater than are generally realized. A teacher can meet this responsibility and plan adequate instruction accordingly only through a careful analysis of the students and through a continuing deep interest in them.

Adequate Standards of Performance

Business and industry demands adequate performance as a condition of continued employment. Professional teachers continually evaluate their own effectiveness and the standard of learning achieved by the students. The desire to maintain pleasant personal relationships with the students must not cause the acceptance of a low level of learning or performance. It is a fallacy to believe that accepting lower standards to please a student will affect a genuine improvement in the student-teacher relationship. Good teachers are remembered in later years but are not necessarily liked while they are teaching. Reasonable standards strictly enforced are not resented by earnest students, and they will thank you later.

Teachers fail to provide competent instruction when they permit their students to get by with a substandard performance, or without thoroughly learning information pertinent to safe and effective performance on the job.

Positive Emphasis

Teachers have a tremendous influence on their students' image of education and the occupation that is being taught. The way teachers conduct themselves, the attitudes they display, and the manner in which they develop their instruction all contribute to the formation of either *positive* or *negative* impressions by their students.

Most new teachers tend to adopt the teaching methods used when they were students. These methods may or may not have been good or effective. Remember the awful teacher you had? Which of their practices influenced you positively? Which negatively? Did your good teachers frame comments and instructions in a pleasant, positive fashion? It is a safe bet that the good teachers "talked up" the subject, your ability to master it, and the pleasant consequences for doing so. In a word, those good teachers probably had a passion for what they were doing. The teacher you have a negative impression of may have used sarcasm and lots of threats about what would happen if you didn't do something. With few exceptions, negative teaching results in negative learning. The professional teacher accentuates the positive.

Caring

Really good teachers are distinguished by one overriding characteristic: they care about their students, their subject, and teaching and learning. They are interested in the well-being of all aspects of their program. They want their students to succeed, and they want their occupation to be bettered by the addition of the students they are preparing. The caring teacher steps back and remembers what it was like to be a student. The caring teacher knows that students need the teacher, not so much for the answers, but for guidance as to what the questions are.

Just as caring teachers produce graduates who care about their work, uncaring teachers produce uncaring graduates. A caring attitude or behavior cannot be learned or purchased. If the adage "Nobody cares how much you know until they know how much you care" is true, the ultimate success of teachers lies in their caring.

Summary

This chapter has addressed some of the students' needs and their relationship to each other. These needs may be arranged in a hierarchical order as suggested by Abraham Maslow. Some principles of teaching that are drawn from the principles of learning were described. Ideas for developing a healthful climate for learning were discussed, and a number of traits of professional teachers were described.

For Further Reading

Beck, L.G. (1994). *Reclaiming Educational Administration as a Caring Profession.* New York: Teachers College Press.

Board, J.C. (1992). *A Special Relationship: Our Teachers and How We Learned.* Wainscott, NY: Pushcart Press.

Breckenridge, E. (1976, December). "Improving School Climate." *Phi Delta Kappan. 58*(4), 314–318.

Caine, R.N., and Caine, G. (1991). *Making Connections: Teaching and the Human Brain.* Alexandria, VA: Association for Supervision and Curriculum Development.

Curwin, R.L., and Mendler, A.N. (1989). *Discipline With Dignity.* Alexandria, VA: Association for Supervision and Curriculum Development.

Darling-Hammond, L. (1988). "Accountability and Teacher Professionalism." *American Educator* 12(4): 8–13.

Freedman, S.G. (1990). *Small Victories: The Real World of a Teacher, Her Students and Their High School.* New York: Harper and Row.

Wittrock, M. (Ed.) (1986). *Handbook of Research on Teaching.* New York: Macmillan.

Professional Resources

American Vocational Association, Products Department, 1410 King Street, Alexandria, VA 22314, (800) 826–9972.

Association for Supervision and Curriculum Development, 1250 N. Pitt Street, Alexandria, VA 22314–1453; (703) 549–9110; e-mail **member@ascd.org**

Crisis Prevention Institute, 3315 North 124th Street, Brookfield, WI 53005; (800) 558–8976.

Discussion Questions

1. Why is it important to be aware of "where students are from" in terms of their physical and psychological comfort?

2. How can we distinguish physical needs from emotional needs?

3. What practical purpose does the establishment of a climate of learning serve?

4. What is *professionalism*? Why is it so important that teachers act and perform in a professional manner?

5. How does the teacher's attitude affect learning in the classroom?

Exercises

1. Name and explain the meaning of each of the levels of needs as suggested by Maslow.

    a. _____ which means _____

    _____

    b. _____ which means _____

    _____

    c. _____ which means _____

    _____

    d. _____ which means _____

    _____

    e. _____ which means _____

2. Name seven rules for establishing a healthful climate for learning and give an example of how you would implement them in teaching your occupation.

    a. _____ implemented by _____

    _____

    _____

    b. _____ implemented by _____

    _____

    _____

    c. _____ implemented by _____

    _____

    _____

    d. _____ implemented by _____

    _____

    _____

    e. _____ implemented _____

    _____

    _____

    _____

    f. _____ implemented _____

    _____

    _____

    g. _____ implemented _____

    _____

    _____

3. List the basic traits of a professional teacher and briefly explain what each consists of.

a. _____ consisting of _____
   _____
   _____

b. _____ consisting of _____
   _____
   _____

c. _____ consisting of _____
   _____
   _____

d. _____ consisting of _____
   _____
   _____

e. _____ consisting of _____
   _____

f. _____ consisting of_____
   _____
   _____

g. _____ consisting of _____
   _____
   _____

h. _____ consisting of _____
   _____
   _____

i. _____ consisting of _____
   _____
   _____

j. _____ consisting of _____
   _____
   _____

k. _____ consisting of _____
   _____
   _____

5 Helping Your Horse Keep Up with the Cart

Techniques for Organizing Your Course

DO YOU EVER FEEL that your job or your life is rushing along and that you are just barely able to keep up? Many teachers of occupational subjects—often having been hired on Friday to begin teaching Monday—find themselves in that predicament. The first Saturday and Sunday are spent getting ready for Monday, and the next few nights are spent preparing for the succeeding day. Weekends are spent trying to get a few days ahead. These new teachers first try this, then that, learning a little from each experience. Sooner or later, most of them develop a system that works. The manner by which many people become teachers of occupational subjects dictates some of this trial-and-error teaching; but much pain and many mistakes can be avoided by adopting a system of instruction that has already been developed, tried, and tested, and then waiting to experiment after some practice has been gained.

The instructional process, or system, that is described here has been designed for, refined, and used with groups, but the teacher must always keep in mind that groups are composed of individuals, who learn in their own way and for their own reasons. Although we usually teach a group, the learning that takes place is individual learning.

The Instructional Process

The process of organizing a course and committing it to paper for action in the classroom is known as curriculum development. The process that is shown in Figure 5.1 and explained below will produce an educational program that is derived from actual job requirements and that will prepare students to succeed after employment. Figure 5.1 is a representation of the entire instructional process. Several steps in that process are treated in this text with chapters of their own but are included in this chapter for the sake of clarity.

Before a teacher, an advisory group, or a curriculum developer begins developing a course or program or revising an existing program, they should determine the scope, or mission, of the program. If the course or program is to be focused on preparing individuals for specific jobs, it may be markedly different from one that is focused on preparing people to assume entry level positions in a cluster of jobs. Once these basic questions are answered, program development can begin in earnest.

Needs Assessment

The first step in organizing an occupational course and developing curriculum is to conduct a *needs assessment*. *Need* simply refers to a measurable difference between what exists and what is desired. In other words, what do the students know and what are they able to do, and what do they have to know or do in order to successfully perform on the job?

A detailed examination of the methods of conducting a needs assessment is beyond the scope of this book, but brief descriptions of the major steps follow.

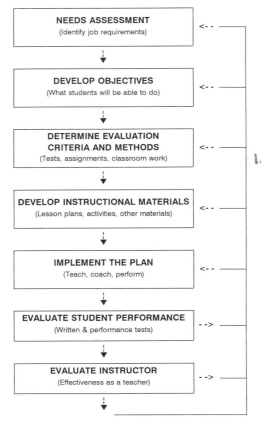

Figure 5.1   The Instructional Process

(The bibliography section contains a list of publications that will be helpful in conducting needs assessments.) Most needs assessments begin with a determination of what job holders do at work. This determination is called *job analysis*.

1. *Job Analysis.* A job analysis is a listing, in performance sequence, of the steps or processes of a job or task. This list also contains the safety measures, the frequency with which each task is performed, its importance to other tasks, technical information, and procedures concerned with its accomplishment. A job analysis usually includes a list of tools, machines, instruments, and materials used in completing the job. A job analysis is specific: it refers to one particular job or to related tasks that are usually assigned to one individual.

Most teachers, having just left an occupation, can list the major tasks of their job in a very short time. This list of major tasks serves as the basis for the overall goals of a course. For example, automobile mechanics often perform tune-ups; computer technicians diagnose hardware problems; nurses provide patient care; cosmetologists style hair; carpenters frame walls; and sales persons ring-up merchandise. Each of these activities is a major task performed on the job, and the goal would be to provide instruction so that graduates can perform these tasks. The job analysis provides an understanding of the tasks involved in each job by providing all data that are relevant to the job. Job analyses are checked and revised frequently in order to remain up-to-date with materials and technology. For this reason, it is advisable to have persons who are presently working on a job check any job analyses that you perform for accuracy. A subject matter advisory committee can help you with this latter activity.

Once all major job tasks are listed through the use of job analysis, a task analysis can be completed. A job analysis may already have been done that is appropriate for the instructional program. Large school districts, the military services, and state departments of education are good sources of job analyses, as are apprentice training programs.

2. *Task Analysis.*   Task analysis is the process of synthesizing the knowledge and skills required to perform the tasks that were identified in the job analysis. A task generally requires some combination of skills and knowledge, that is, it requires both physical and mental action on the part of the worker. Each task has a definite starting and stopping point and has two or more steps. Jobs usually consist of a series of interdependent tasks, and the tasks would normally be completed in proper sequence if the job is to be done satisfactorily. Tasks, which are the smallest units of job activity having a specific purpose, comprise the step-by-step process of completing a job.

One task that is common to many occupations is "select materials." In order to carry out this task, the employee needs to have some specific skills and knowledge, such as knowing the source of the materials and their location, how to select the correct material, and how to measure the proper quantity.

Many people "record data" on the job—another task. To be able to complete this task, an employee must be able to accurately transfer information from one source to another, including all details, and make legible notes.

Research and actual experience are in agreement that while cognitive and manipulative (knowing and doing) skills are essential to any job or task, a basic part of job success falls on the affective factors—values and attitudes. Skills and knowledge are relatively easy to identify, but the values and attitudes that make up the affective domain are not. Surveys of employees have found that job success is most often dependent on the values and attitudes that a person brings to the job. These values and attitudes, along with the skills and knowledge needed, must be identified so that they can be considered in the learning process. These three areas, attitudes, manipulative skills, and knowledge, will be elaborated upon in the next section.

Completing a task analysis is a complex, time-consuming process, and one that should not be undertaken lightly. The knowledge and skill components of most tasks are fairly obvious once the task is listed, so tasks should not be over-analyzed in the name of thoroughness. "Nice-to-know" and trivial information such as "pick up the scalpel" should not be included in the task analysis. Novice teachers are advised to consult with state department of education personnel for assistance. Several other resources for job and task analyses include textbooks, shop manuals, procedure sheets, and technical bulletins from manufacturers.

Develop Performance Objectives

A great amount of effort goes into performing job and task analyses. Once developed, these two analyses are the source for performance objectives. The performance objectives, in turn, reveal a great many factors about what should be taught, in what sequence, and how.

A performance objective is a statement of one of the things a student will be able to do upon completion of instruction. Student performance objectives are developed from the skills, knowledge, and attitudes that were revealed as necessary for job success in the job and task analyses.

Performance objectives are also commonly known as behavioral objectives (because they express behavior changes desired), observable objectives (because we can see changes that occur), measurable objectives (because we can measure the change that has occurred), and terminal objectives (because they express a desired end behavior).

By whatever name you call them, meaningful student performance objectives are stated in terms of expected student behavior at the end of the learning period. When these objectives are precisely stated and have been made available to the students prior to and during instruction, they are more likely to be able to perform in the manner desired. Tests and other means of evaluation of the students' progress tell both the instructor and the students to what extent they both have been successful in achieving the student performance objectives.

 A student performance objective consists of three basic elements: (1) the *action* that the students must be capable of performing, (2) the *conditions* under which they are expected to perform, and (3) the *standards* of performance they must reach. By describing each element in detail, an explicit and measurable performance objective is created. The *action* or performance element describes an observable end-of-instruction behavior. This is the skill, knowledge, or attitude that the student must be able to demonstrate. It can best be determined by asking, What will the students be able to do?

The *conditions* element, which is derived from the task analysis, should simulate, to the maximum extent possible, actual job conditions. This element should also include the tools, equipment, references, materials, and guides required in the performance of the task and the supervision and assistance available. These latter items are often called the "givens" because we tell the student in the objective what they will be given to perform the activity described in the first element.

The *standards* element of a performance objective states how well the student must be able to perform the task. It describes minimum acceptable performance, sets a time limit where applicable, or it defines quality and quantity standards for the product or service produced.

One style of objective writing calls for the objective to answer, Who does what, at (or in) what time, under what conditions, in what amount, and measured by what method?

The *who* in the question relates to the person or persons who are to perform an activity. For example:

1. All students . . .
2. Each participant . . .

When writing performance objectives, it should be obvious that the *who* usually relates to students, and may eventually be eliminated as unnecessary use of ink and paper. As you begin to write objectives, though, always include reference to the *who.*

The *does what* (the performance expected) relates to that which is to be known or done as a result of the course, unit, or program for example:

1. Will be able to *list* the various parts of . . .
2. Will *demonstrate* a desire to . . .
3. Will be able to *manipulate* the controls on the sphygmomanometer . . .

The *time* relates to (1) the specific time in which the task will have been learned, or (2) the time that is allowed to perform the task on the job. For example,

1. At completion of the course . . .
2. Within thirty minutes . . .
3. By the second semester of the 12th grade . . .

The *under what conditions* segment of the question relates to the situation in which the learning will take place.

1. In an actual work situation . . .
2. In a supervised classroom environment . . .
3. With the body submerged under at least 10 feet of water . . .
4. In the Vocational Education for Special Needs Program . . .

The *in what amount* relates to the minimum level to be achieved or the criterion for success. Example phrases include:

1. Sixteen of the 18 muscles . . .
2. Three of the four major causes of failure . . .
3. At least twice . . .

The *measured by what method* relates to the techniques used for assessing successful completion of the actions required in the objective. Some measuring techniques can be expressed in these ways:

1. As evidenced by 50 of 60 correct answers on a multiple choice examination . . .
2. As observed by the teacher . . .
3. As indicated by student personnel records . . .
4. According to the Uniform Building Code . . .

An example of a student performance objective for this chapter might read as follows.

Upon completion of this unit of instruction, all students (who), when given a list of action verbs denoting performance in their occupation (under what conditions), will be able to write at least ten student performance objectives in each of the three behavioral domains (does what). At least twenty-five (in what amount) of the objectives when compared to a rubric will contain all answers to the questions: Who, does what, in what time, under what conditions, in what amount, and measured by what method? (as measured by)

Example phrases for the three basic elements of a performance objective follow.

Action (or performance)

The student will label the sketches . . .
The student will describe the preparation of . . .
The student will prepare the surface . . .
The student will inspect five welds . . .
The student will identify five facial shapes . . .
The student will type the . . .
The student will remove and replace the . . .

Conditions (or givens)

Random samples of automotive parts . . .
State Board of Nurse Examiner's Regulations . . .
A list of hard woods . . .
Samples of type faces . . .
An electronic schematic . . .
A supply of do-dads . . .
Appropriate reference manuals . . .

Standards

Accurate to the nearest whole number . . .
Without error. . .
Five out of eight times . . .
Within plus or minus two degrees . . .
So that it meets some specific standard, such as licensing, etc . . .

Examples of completed performance objectives may be found in the exercises section at the end of this chapter. Good performance objectives are (1) relevant—they are converted directly from a specific task or task element; (2) complete—they contain an action statement, conditions, and standards; (3) precise—they are stated so explicitly that there can be no misunderstanding; and (4) measurable—the standards include a means for measuring when and the degree to which the objective has been achieved.

Before the discussion continues on the instructional process as depicted in Figure 5.1, it is necessary to take a side trip and discuss the so-called domains in which learning takes place and the relationship of those domains to student performance objectives.

Learning Domains

As we have seen, educational theorists have identified three major domains in which learning occurs—the *cognitive*, the *affective*, and the *psychomotor*. Each domain is further broken into levels of learning that go from the simple to the complex. These levels are related to the three levels of learning that were discussed in Chapter 3 and are compared to those levels later in this section.

Cognitive Domain. This domain deals with knowledge and intellectual learning. A student performance objective requiring a student to calculate the cost of a product would fall into the cognitive domain, as would one that requires a student to describe a process. Behaviors in the cognitive domain usually deal with knowing something, and rarely require any manipulation beyond writing or speaking. Following is a list of terms that may be used to write objectives at the various levels of the cognitive domain. Remember, the lower the level, the simpler the objective. Most objectives, except at the very beginning of a course or program, should be written to the mid and upper levels. In developing objectives, it is important to remember the level that students must achieve to be successful on the job.

Level 1: Knowledge
define
memorize
repeat
list
recall
name
relate

Level 2: Comprehension
restate
discuss
describe
recognize
explain
express
identify
locate
report
review
tell

Level 3: Application
translate
interpret
apply
employ
use
demonstrate
dramatize
practice
illustrate
operate
schedule
shop
sketch

Level 4: Analysis
distinguish   question
differentiate   relate
analyze   solve
appraise   examine
calculate
experiment
test
compare
contrast
criticize
diagram
inspect
debate
inventory

Level 5: Synthesis
compose
plan
propose
design
formulate
arrange
collect
assemble

Level 6: Evaluation
judge
appraise
evaluate
rate
compute
value
revise
score

Level 5: Synthesis
construct
create
set up
organize
manage
prepare

Level 6: Evaluation
select
choose
assess
estimate
measure

Affective Domain.   The affective domain deals with attitudes, values, feelings, and emotions. It is nearly impossible to measure directly what a person is feeling, so when writing objectives in the affective domain, we have to seek behaviors that will indicate the feelings or attitudes of the students. For example, a student who (without being prompted) always wears safety glasses, uses the proper guards, and follows safety rules is demonstrating a positive attitude toward safety. A positive attitude toward punctuality or responsibility might be demonstrated by a student who always arrives for class on time and gets right to work.

As in the cognitive domain, the affective domain has been subdivided into levels. It is important to remember that higher level tasks are not necessarily more difficult. Instead, they demonstrate a deeper understanding and mastery of the subject. Obviously, within operating constraints, we want our students to learn to as high a level as practical for success on the job.

Here is a lists of terms for the five levels in the affective domain that might be used to describe desired behavior.

Level 1: Receiving
observe
be conscious
realize
be sensitive
attend to
listen
discriminate
be alert
remember
prefer

Level 2: Responding
willing
comply
obey
look
engage
display
practice
respond
perform

Level 3: Valuing
continue to desire
grow
feel
participate
assume responsibility
enable
initiate
examine
influence
accept
prefer
assume

Level 4: Organizing the Values
crystallize
form judgment
relate
weigh
be realistic
judge
regulate

cooperate
contribute
volunteer
exhibit
consider
participate
extend
enrich
explore

Level 5: Characterization by a Value or Value Complex
ready
revise
view
approach
plan
arrive
rely
find
examine
judge
be consistent
be conscientious

When measuring performance in the affective domain, it is often necessary for the teacher to rely on check lists of desired behavior and to closely (often unobtrusively) observe student behavior.

Psychomotor Domain. The psychomotor domain deals with physical skills such as typing, pounding a nail, and manipulating instruments. The psychomotor domain has four levels, with the lowest requiring the simple imitation of the teacher's actions. (One theorist has divided the psychomotor domain into five levels, another has identified seven.)

At the higher levels in the psychomotor domain, the student can apply the learned skills in new situations. A list of terms that may be used for writing performance objectives in the various levels of the psychomotor domain follows.

Level 1: Observation	Level 2: Imitation
find	build
locate	demonstrate
observe	express
recognize	measure
sort	operate
	perform
	play
	mend
	use
	construct
	draw
	run

Level 3: Practice	*Level 4: Adaptation*
build	adapt
demonstrate	administer
express	create
measure	manipulate
operate	plan
perform	produce
play	promote
write	regulate
construct	research
run	teach
use	construct
	draw
	mend

A Note on Words Used.   You may have noticed that some of the same words appeared on the three lists, and, in some cases, they appeared on the same list at different levels. That is because these words either indicate some type of behavior common to two or more of the domains or a skill that can be achieved at different levels. Always keep in mind the final behavior that you wish the students to demonstrate. Think carefully about whether they will be required to use their intellect alone, their feelings or emotions, or whether they will have to perform some physical manipulation. One last list of words—this one a <u>do not use</u> list—follows.

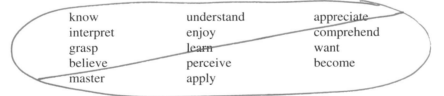

know	understand	appreciate
interpret	enjoy	comprehend
grasp	learn	want
believe	perceive	become
master	apply	

Use of any of these words will lead to a vague and ambiguous student performance objective. Performance has to be described as an observable action. It is difficult to observe or measure *understanding*. How, for example, does a teacher know when a student knows something? The words in the other three lists are less ambiguous because they provide examples of behavior that is immediately observable. In addition, they are more easily measured through the use of objective evaluation devices such as tests or checklists.

Relationship of Domains.   The three domains, while classified separately, are not mutually exclusive. A single objective may require a student to demonstrate learning that has occurred in more than one domain. For example, if the students were required to manufacture a product, they would need to demonstrate psychomotor skills in the manufacturing, cognitive skills in calculating needed materials, and affective values in a demonstrated appreciation of quality workmanship. Yet one single psychomotor objective could cover the process—All students will be able to manufacture a thingamajig . . .

Since most of occupational education is skill-oriented, our objectives are primarily psychomotor. This means that one objective, while on the surface indicating manipulative behavior, also will include behavior in the cognitive and affective domains. After all, in order to perform a skill, we need to know a number of things (such as the correct procedure, materials, and processes) and we need to appreciate some things (such as quality work, empathy, etc.), in addition to the physical act of doing what we are doing.

The relationship of the several domains and the various levels to teaching activities will be discussed in more detail in the next chapter. For now, it is necessary to relate the three *levels of learning* described in Chapter 3 to the three *learning domains* and their associated levels. Figure 5.2 contains a graphic description of the relationship of the performance objectives to the level of learning.

You will recall that there are three basic levels of learning: general, working, and qualified. These three levels are roughly comparable to levels in the three domains. Figure 5.2 contains the three levels toward which we gear instruction and the levels from the several domains that approximate them.

The strength of the students' motivation and the quality of their performance are directly related to their knowing exactly what they have to do and to knowing how well they have performed when they have finished. Performance objectives should not only be shared with the students, but they should be fully explained prior to instruction.

Clear and detailed performance objectives are the first step toward a sound, logical, organized course. Performance objectives allow the teacher to see, well in advance, what instructional strategies will best help students achieve desired job behavior. (The exercises at the end of this chapter provide examples of student performance objectives and some practice activities in writing them.)

LEVEL 1:
GENERAL KNOWLEDGE

LEVEL 2:
WORKING KNOWLEDGE

LEVEL 3:
QUALIFIED KNOWLEDGE

	Cognitive Domain	Affective Domain	Psychomotor Domain
General	Knowledge Comprehension	Receiving	Observation Initiation
Working (With Supervision)	Application Analysis	Responding Valuing	Practicing
Qualified (Without Supervision)	Synthesis Evaluation	Characterization by a Value or Value Complex	Adaptation

Figure 5.2 *The Relationship of Performance Objectives to Levels of Learning*

Determining Evaluation Criteria and Methods

This step in the instructional process involves deciding how you will determine whether the students have learned anything as a result of your instruction. It might seem strange at first to develop evaluation criteria and methods *before* you have even seen the students, but it is actually a crucial step often overlooked or minimized. Because very few of us can read others' minds, it becomes necessary to plan for the criteria and methods that we will use to determine the amount and type of learning that has taken place. If the student performance objectives have been developed from the requirements of the job and have been correctly stated, they will tell us the exact method we will need to use to evaluate the learning and the level of learning that will be satisfactory. The objectives will usually even be specific enough to state, for example, in the cognitive domain, that students will be able to correctly answer X number of questions on a multiple-choice test, or that they will be able to perform some manipulative activity within a given amount of time and to some particular level. The techniques for developing tests are briefly covered in a later chapter, but for the purposes here, it is necessary to know that the teacher has to think about and plan for them in advance.

Organizing the Lessons

The Four-Step System

A system of instruction for producing individual learning in a group setting has been developed that capitalizes on what has been learned through research on what motivates people, how the senses are used to receive information, and how the mind works to retain and transfer skills and knowledges. In essence, there are four steps in this system : (1) motivating the students; (2) presenting information to them; (3) application of what has been presented; and (4) evaluation according to some standard or criterion. In plain English, this means that each item of instruction, by whatever method or technique that it is taught, should create an interest in the learner, teach a skill or provide information, allow for practice in its use, and determine the degree to which it has been learned. Instruction is not complete or effective unless the four steps are followed.

Obviously this four-step instructional system cannot be used without preparation, so it could be argued that the act of instruction is actually composed of five steps—the first being preparation by the teacher. Preparation includes such things as determination and analysis of what is needed to be taught (curriculum development); analysis and planning of the most effective learning activity; the gathering or preparation of the necessary tools, materials, and media; and the arrangement of the facilities for the most effective learning environment. Preparation must be done for each of the four steps in the system.

The four step system is explained in the following paragraphs. Later, you will learn how the four-step process is committed to writing in the form of a lesson plan.

Step 1–Motivation

The motivation step of the instructional process has the purpose of focusing the learners' attention on what is to be taught. Motivation is probably the most critical of the steps, for if the learners are not motivated, the rest of the process may fail. The teacher's first concern when starting group instruction is to redirect and focus attention on the matter to be studied. When it is remembered that one is continually facing a diverse group, it presents quite a challenge to the imagination, skill, and showmanship of the teacher.

There are many techniques for motivating students, but three essentials should always be considered: (1) focus attention on the lesson; (2) generate enthusiasm; and (3) demonstrate the lesson's relevance to the learners' lives.

Focusing attention on the teacher and the topic can be done in many ways. Often, just taking your usual position and standing silently may get attention, after which the topic can be announced. Sometimes, unrolling a chart, writing a word on the chalkboard, holding up an object, or switching on an overhead projector will serve to focus attention. It is rare that the same attention-getting technique will work all the time. In fact, sometimes using the same technique may be to your detriment. Remember, variety *is* the spice of life. Add some to your class.

The second essential element of the motivation step is enthusiasm. At the risk of overusing the cliché, enthusiasm is contagious. If the teacher is not enthused, the students will have difficulty conjuring up any interest or enthusiasm of their own. Teacher enthusiasm is revealed in many ways: by thorough preparation; imaginative treatment of the subject; obvious pleasure in the presentation of the subject; and dynamic action and animated conversation. If the teacher looks upon the lesson or the subject as a necessary evil or a dull duty, the outcome in terms of learning is doubtful. In real life, some subjects are boring to the teacher. That is where imagination and creativity are important. Find a guest speaker, or use a film, or make up a game, but do something that will keep the enthusiasm high.

The third element of successful motivation is relevance. Students need to know how the lesson to be learned relates to what they will learn in the future and to what they have learned in the past. This relationship should be demonstrated in as positive a fashion as possible and should be tied to employment and success in the occupation being learned. Avoid statements such as, "If you don't learn this, you won't be able to do that." Use the positive form; "If you learn this well, your job will be much easier to perform." Relate incidents from your own experience or that of others. Ask students questions that will lead them to state the importance in their own words. Show pictures, outlines, films, videos, or perform a demonstration, but the end result must be that students see the relevance of the subject to their eventual success. A point to remember—whenever the teacher observes lagging interest, at whatever point during lesson, it is time to remotivate by refocusing and bringing the lesson into perspective.

Step 2—Presentation

Although the techniques of presentation are discussed in detail in the next chapter, a few highlights will be noted here. The purpose of this step is to present instruction in order that the students can learn a new skill or concept. This is where the teacher brings before the students words, actions, pictures, symbols, concepts, and sounds for consideration. Uninitiated critics view this as a *pouring in* or *injecting* of knowledge. In reality, it is a process of assisting the students in absorbing, receiving, and assimilating the material. The emphasis in this step is on learning rather than on teaching. A good presentation requires clear purpose (objectives) and logically organized facts or ideas. Proper pacing of the material to suit the majority of the group is a necessity. Supplementary provisions should be made for fast or slow students. Feedback from the students during the presentation is essential. Questioning the students sustains interest (remotivates them) while also providing an indication of the degree of their understanding.

Step 3—Application

The application step provides opportunity for the student to put into use the skill, information, or ideas that have been presented. Laboratories and practice equipment are provided for this purpose. Although no sensible person would expect to teach a skill without application in the form of practice, this step is sometimes overlooked or underemphasized by inexperienced teachers.

Learners should be provided with the opportunity to apply new knowledge and skill as quickly as possible. This is not easy to accomplish in many teaching/learning situations. Good teachers, however, plan the application step more carefully than any other. They recognize the importance of quickly providing all learners with the opportunity to use a new skill or knowledge. *Use* is the key concept in application. Application is not a one-shot process, particularly with respect to skills. Initial application may be arranged coincident with or immediately after presentation, but there may be a need for constant practice and application in order to achieve perfection in many skills.

Step 4—Evaluation

Evaluation means to place a value upon, to judge, or to rate. Overall evaluation of student progress throughout a course is the ultimate aim, but evaluation as a step in the teaching process refers to the judgment or rating of each separate activity or unit of instruction.

The obvious technique for evaluation is, of course, some type of testing. In occupational education classes, evaluation should be based primarily upon observation of performance and the results of performance (a finished product, for example). Construction of tests to measure this is discussed in Chapter 7. Peer- and self-assessment are also techniques that can be used as part of the evaluation step. In regard to details or small bits of learning, evaluation can be accomplished by assessing student reaction to oral questions. Careful observation of students is essential because even facial expressions may reveal understanding or confusion.

Although evaluation is studied here as one step in the instructional process, in practice it should be a *series* of checks on progress extending through all the major steps of instruction. In such continuous evaluation, questions may be skillfully used during the introductory or motivation phase of the instruction to arouse and to focus attention. Through the presentation step, questions and problems may be used to check on understanding, step by step, as the explanation is given or the demonstration is made. More questions may be used during the application or laboratory phase to help gain a greater insight or to analyze the application of the work to different materials or under different circumstances. In the final analysis, performance tests should be given and ratings made on laboratory exercises or tasks in order to evaluate success in occupational classes and to check on the effectiveness of the instruction.

The four steps of instruction, then, are *motivation, presentation, application,* and *evaluation.* Successful teachers plan and conduct all of their instruction based on these four steps. From a teaching standpoint, the system allows for incorporation of all the salient learning theories and principles of learning and instruction. The system is graphically portrayed in Figure 5.3.

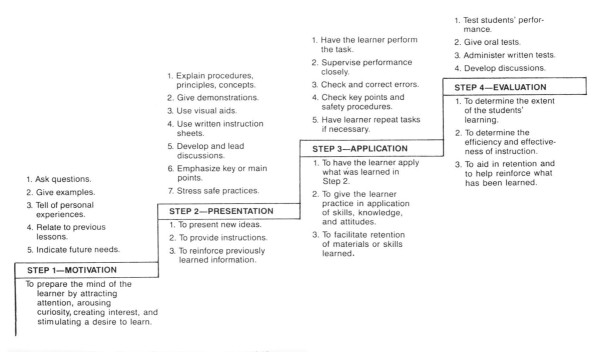

Figure 5.3 The Four-Step Instructional Process

The Lesson Plan

A lesson plan is a guide to the presentation of a unit of instruction. Instructional units are related to the task and job analyses that are conducted for program development. Often one task will be taught using one lesson. In other cases, one lesson may cover several tasks. Sometimes one lesson will be used to provide the background necessary to learn a task or group of tasks. The lesson plan serves as the teacher's road map in the classroom. In addition to an outline and the material to be presented, the lesson plan specifies the procedures the teacher intends to follow in presenting it and lists all materials and equipment needed. A good lesson plan is neither a crutch nor an impediment. A good lesson plan serves as an aid to the instructor because, if followed, it ensures that all material required to meet the lesson objectives will be presented in the most effective order and be enlivened by carefully chosen anecdotes, questions, and instructional aids. Use of a lesson plan does not preclude minor adjustments, either in procedure or subject matter, which must be made to suit varying situations. Lesson planning is anticipatory teaching. It requires a comprehensive understanding of the subject matter, knowledge of the background and ability of the students, a thorough comprehension of the principles of learning and teaching, familiarity with acceptable and effective teaching techniques, and a constant awareness of the objectives and their application.

Lesson plans take many forms, so it is a good idea to adopt a format and stick with it for all lessons you prepare. The format that is illustrated and explained here is adapted from one required of instructors in the U.S. Army Service Schools. A complete first and second page Instructor's Lesson Plan may be found in the appendix. Enlarge those pages to 8½" by 11" paper and have a quick-print shop print about 200 copies. Fill them out by hand at first, but as you gain proficiency, type (or word process) them and keep them in a three-ring binder.

The various sections of the Instructor's Lesson Plan (Figure 5.4) are explained in the following paragraphs. A completed Lesson Plan is shown in the Appendixes.

Subject

The *subject* is the name of the unit of instruction of which this lesson is a part. Examples would include Framing, Terminology, Prosthetics, Resistive Circuits, or any other comprehensive topic. The name of the course is usually *not* what is referred to in the subject space.

Title of Lesson

The title of the lesson is the name of the specific procedure or body of knowledge that is to be taught in this particular lesson. From carpentry, a lesson might be Framing Doors; from nursing, Subcutaneous Injections; from electronics, Calculating Voltage Gains; and from automobile mechanics, Relining Brakes.

INSTRUCTOR'S LESSON PLAN		
SUBJECT:	**INSTRUCTOR:**	
TITLE OF LESSON:		
TIME PERIOD (TOTAL):		
TYPE OF LESSON:		
PLACE:		
TRAINING AIDS:		
OBJECTIVE(S):		
INSTRUCTOR REFERENCES:		
STUDENT REFERENCES AND HOMEWORK:		
TIME	**LESSON OUTLINE**	**KEY POINTS AND AID CUES**

Figure 5.4   Instructor's Lesson Plan

Time Period

The time periods for lessons vary. A lesson might be any length from several minutes to several hours or longer. But remember, a lesson isn't complete unless the elements of motivation, presentation, application, and evaluation are included.

Type of Lesson

This section refers to whether the lesson is primarily a lecture, demonstration, field trip, or other instructional technique. (The various techniques are discussed in Chapter 6.) The type of learning objective will usually dictate the most appropriate method to use.

Place

The place where the lesson will take place could be in the classroom, the shop or laboratory, on-the-job, in the field, at a hospital, or any number of other places. If more than one facility is needed, indicate it.

Training Aids

What material assistance is needed to teach the lesson? The models, pieces of equipment, films, slides, or handouts that the teacher and students will use are listed in this section.

Objectives

The objectives listed here must unquestionably contribute to accomplishing one or more of the objectives for the course and for the unit of which the lesson is a part. These objectives should be specific and stated in terms of measurable or observable student behavior. In other words, they are student performance objectives. Lesson objectives serve as the controlling element for the method of instruction, the depth and scope of subject matter, and the nature of the examination that is used to evaluate student performance. Lesson objectives specify what the students must know or do, how well they have to know it, and how well they will demonstrate the knowledge or skill. The word *demonstrate* is important, for how will we know whether the students can do what is required unless we can see it? If you are still not sure if your objectives are workable, re-read the section at the beginning of this chapter, consult any of the references, and perform the self-check exercises at the end of the chapter. Many instructors place the objectives in the introduction of the lesson and share them directly with the students as part of the lesson.

Instructor References

This section should contain a list of the books, articles, technical publications, or other materials that you will use to prepare for and refer to during the lesson. List everything needed so that the next time the lesson is given there will not be needless searching for it.

Student References and Homework

Chapters of books to be read, assignments to be completed or handed in, and any other student references or homework are listed in this section.

Lesson Outline

Once the information to be presented in a lesson has been gathered, there are several ways of organizing it. The guiding question should always be, Which order of presentation will best suit the stage of instruction, the subject matter itself, student abilities, course objectives, and the time and facilities available? There are four common methods of organizing the facts for a lesson: (1) the chronological order, (2) the spatial order, (3) the logical order, and (4) the psychological order.

Chronological order refers to time. The time order, which is very easy to follow, is best suited to an explanation of process, procedure, or the discussion of the historical aspects of a subject.

When using the *spatial order*, details are arranged according to their location, such as from near to far, inside to outside, and from right to left. This method is particularly useful when explaining assembly processes or demonstrating the use of machines or instruments.

Chronological and spatial orders exist in nature, *logical order* does not. Facts to be presented are arranged in some logical order according to a plan worked out by the teacher. Facts move from cause to effect, from the least important to the most important, or from the general to the specific. Logical order, which is used in this book, is the most commonly used method of organizing material.

Psychological order is used most often with newly introduced subjects. Using this method, a natural sequence of instruction, based on common experiences, is used. Instruction proceeds from the known to the unknown.

By whichever method it is organized, a lesson plan should include (1) an opening statement or introduction to stimulate motivation and interest, a statement of the objectives in behavioral terms, and a tie-in to previous lessons or to life experiences of the students; (2) a topical outline of the subject matter in the order that it is to be presented; (3) provision for application of the material presented; and (4) the evaluative measures to be used during instruction.

Introduction. This section of the lesson plan is most closely related to the motivation phase of the instructional system described previously. The Introduction should serve several purposes: to establish common ground between the teacher and the students, to capture and hold the attention of the group, to indicate what will be covered during the presentation and to relate this to the entire course, to point out specific benefits the student can expect from the learning, and finally, to establish a receptive attitude toward the subject and lead into the presentation stage. The introduction is best used as the motivation step to set the stage for learning.

An effective way to begin a lesson is to tell a story that relates to the subject and establishes a background for developing learning results. Students' attention might be gained by making an unexpected or surprising statement or by asking a question that helps relate the lesson topic to the needs of the group.

The primary purpose of the introduction in the lesson plan is to document for the students specific reasons for needing to be familiar with, to know, to understand, to apply, or to be able to perform what they are about to learn. This motivation exercise should be done in a positive fashion, it should appeal to each student personally, and it should accentuate the desire to learn.

The introductory, or motivation, stage should also contain an overview that tells the students what will be covered in the period. A clear, concise presentation of the objective and the key ideas will give the students an indication of the path to be followed. The use of good visual aids here often can help picture for the students what they are about to learn.

Stories, jokes, or incidents that do not help the students focus their attention on the lesson objectives should be avoided. The lesson introduction should be short (5 to 10 minutes) and nonapologetic.

Presentation. In this major section of a lesson plan, the subject matter is developed in a manner that helps the students achieve the desired learning outcomes. This is the *main part* of the lesson and is often called the *development,* or the *body* of the lesson. The success of the lesson depends upon the teacher's ability to communicate effectively with the class, so the selection of the organization method (i.e., chronological, logical, etc.) is important. Whichever method is chosen, the column on the right side of the Instructor's Lesson Plan form can be useful. This Key Points and Aid Cues column is for notes to yourself that keep the lesson on track. Your notes might only consist of an asterisk, which means you should emphasize a point, or it might be a specific question you wish to ask students. If you are using visual aids, the column might contain a note to "Show overhead slide number 1." The Key Points column might also contain statistics, page references, comparisons, or any other meaningful example that will strengthen or clarify the lesson. Periodically, such at the end of each major point, you should have a note to yourself in this section to check the students' understanding of the material presented thus far.

Once the presentation phase of a lesson plan is written, it is a good idea to rehearse it. This will build self-confidence and give you a better idea of the time it will take to present the material. You will also gain experience in the mechanics of using notes, visual aids, and other instructional devices.

Beginning teachers usually have no idea of the time that it takes to deliver individual lessons. As you gain experience, you will be able to estimate the time needed. In addition, you will be more aware of time as you progress through the lesson and will be able to adjust as you go, either extending or shortening portions to accommodate the clock. The column on the left side of the form is labelled Time. Use a chronological system that keeps track of the time cumulatively. For example, the lesson starts at 00:00. The development, or presentation section, will start at 00:05 with the beginning of the first main point. If it takes 10 minutes to complete the first major point, the second major point will begin at 00:15, and so on until the lesson is complete. This will allow you to use the lesson plan without confusion several times a day if necessary.

Many people believe that a good teacher teaches without notes. When teaching occupational or technical subjects, this is akin to setting off on a long journey without a road map. A good teacher feels no shame in referring to notes, especially while reciting facts, figures, and numerical values. Do not overdo it though. Nothing is more deadly than reading to students, and nothing will cause them to lose their attention and erode their confidence in you as a teacher faster.

Application. The importance of student performance in the learning process cannot be overstated. Student performance requires the students to act and to do. In order to learn the manipulative skills common to occupational education, students must practice. Time must be allotted, therefore, in the lesson plan for meaningful student activity. Through this activity, the students learn to follow correct procedures and to reach established standards of performance.

The application step should follow as soon as possible after facts are presented or the correct procedure is demonstrated. Quite often students follow along as the teacher performs a demonstration or works a problem during the presentation stage. Immediately thereafter, the teacher should have the students attempt to perform the procedure, coaching them as necessary. All students should be allowed to complete an operation or procedure independently, with supervision and coaching as it is required.

Key points or *aid cues* that are included in the lesson plan for the application phase include questions or check lists of correct procedures, use of tools or instruments, and checks for accuracy or standards of performance. It is important to plan sufficient time for the application phase of a lesson.

Evaluation. Student knowledge or performance is measured and judged in this phase of a lesson. The student displays or demonstrates whatever competence has been gained, and the teacher discovers just how well it has been learned. There are essentially two types of evaluation used in a given lesson. Informal evaluation occurs as the lesson is being taught and questions are asked by the teacher to check student comprehension. These questions are usually oral and are directed to all students in the class. (See Chapter 6 for a discussion of questioning techniques.) Another informal type of evaluation occurs when the teacher watches the class for signs of expressions of comprehension or frustration. These informal types of evaluation occur throughout the lesson.

Formal evaluation methods usually include tests of some sort. Through the use of tests, the teacher is able to require students to perform some skill or manipulation independently or to work through a problem. By using these measurements of student achievement and comparing them against established

"And then, of course, there's the possibility of being just the slightest bit too organized."

by Glen Dives

standards, teachers can determine the degree of student learning and the effectiveness of the instruction. (Chapter 7 is devoted to an explanation of the various types of test questions and procedures for constructing them.)

Summary

Lessons and lesson plans have four major sections: the introduction or motivation step, presentation step, application step, and evaluation step. These sections are derived from what is known about how people learn most effectively, and they model the four-step instructional system.. Lesson plans list all materials needed to teach a class, ideas for motivating students, an organized plan for presenting subject material, provision for practice or application of what was learned, and an indication of the evaluative devices to be used to check on student performance. Lesson plans allow the teacher more freedom to encourage student questions and discussion because the teacher always will have the end objective in mind. As teachers know what their objectives are and prepare complete lesson plans, their confidence in the classroom will increase. If there is a disadvantage to lesson plans, it is that they are intensely personal documents. The organizational method, the cryptic shorthand notes, and the references to personal stories and incidents usually will preclude their use by anyone but the person who has prepared them. An example of a completed lesson plan may be found in the appendix.

For Further Reading

Bloom, B.S., (Ed.) (1984). *Taxonomy of Educational Objectives, Handbook I: Cognitive Domain.* White Plains, New York: Longman.

Blum-Anderson, J. (1992). "Increasing Enrollment in Higher-Level Mathematics Classes through the Affective Domain." *School Science and Mathematics.* 92(8):433–436.

Briggs, L.J. (1984). "Whatever Happened to Motivation and the Affective Domain?" *Educational Technology.* 24(5):33–34.

Finch, C.R., and Crunkilton, J.R. (1989). *Curriculum Development in Vocational and Technical Education.* Third Edition. Boston: Allyn & Bacon.

Fryklund, V.C. (1970). *Occupational Analysis Techniques and Procedures.* New York: Bruce Publishing Company.

Gagne, R.M., and Briggs, L.J. (1974). *Principles of Instructional Design.* New York: Holt, Rinehart and Winston.

Henak, R.M. (1984). *Lesson Planning for Meaningful Variety in Teaching.* Second Edition. Washington, DC: National Education Association.

Krathwohl, D.R., Bloom, B.S., and Masia, B.B. (1964). *Taxonomy of Educational Objectives, Handbook II: Affective Domain.* White Plains, NY: Longman.

Linnell, C.C. (1994). "Facilitating Curriculum Change: Teacher Concerns as a Factor." *Journal of Industrial Teacher Education.* 33(1):93–96.

Mager, R.F. (1962). *Preparing Instructional Objectives.* Palo Alto, CA: Fearon Publishers.

Mager, R.F., and Beach, K.M., Jr. (1967). *Developing Vocational Instruction.* Belmont, CA: Fearon Publishers.

Simpson, E.J. (1966). *The Classification of Objectives, Psychomotor Domain.* Urbana, IL: University of Illinois.

U.S. Department of Labor. (1991). *Dictionary of Occupational Titles.* Fourth Edison, Revised. Washington, DC: U.S. Government Printing Office.

U.S. Department of Labor. (1972). *Handbook for Analyzing Jobs.* Washington, DC: U.S. Government Printing Office.

Discussion Questions

1. If you were trying to show a supervisor that there was a need for a program to teach others your occupation, where would you go for statistics to support your argument? What types of data would you need?

_____

_____

_____

2. Why is it particularly important for teachers of occupational subjects to use a system of curriculum planning that is based on reliable labor market data?

_____

_____

_____

3. Much emphasis is placed on the development and use of student performance objectives. Why?

_____

_____

_____

4. Discuss the four-step instructional process in terms of the importance of completing each step.

_____

_____

_____

5. Is the four-step instructional process applicable to all types of lessons? Discuss.

_____

_____

_____

6. Explain how the curriculum development process is interrelated with instruction and evaluation.

_____

_____

_____

Exercises

1. Survey the want ads in your local or regional newspaper for one week. Count all *different* ads for jobs that graduates of your class or program could fill. Summarize (1) the education required for the jobs, (2) the beginning salary, and (3) the geographic location and working conditions. Can you think of another use for this information other than in curriculum planning? How about using it as a weekly bulletin board display?

   _____

   _____

   _____

2. Each of the following items represents a component of a performance objective. Using the key, place the letter of the correct component in the blank space preceding each item.

   Key: **a.** target audience (who)
   b. behavior or action (does what)
   c. condition of performance (given)
   d. criterion or standard of performance

   _____ 1. "Given a Hilti air powered nailer . . ."
   _____ 2. ". . . operating a mechanical respirator . . ."
   _____ 3. "replace automobile front disc brakes pads."
   _____ 4. "answer correctly 100% of shop safety test questions."
   _____ 5. "an allied health trainee with no . . ."
   _____ 6. "develop a set of working plans for a two-story addition."
   _____ 7. "given a test bench, an ohmmeter, an electrical circuit . . ."
   _____ 8. "complete the task in ten minutes."
   _____ 9. "set a table for a two-course luncheon for . . ."
   _____ 10. "complete the job at a rate of $1\frac{1}{2}$ acres per hour."
   _____ 11. "using a roller coulter."
   _____ 12. "the retail sales trainee."
   _____ 13. "to National Electrical Code standards."
   _____ 14. "compute the amount of fabric needed."
   _____ 15. "be able to verbalize . . ."
   _____ 16. "At least three-fourths of the students . . ."
   _____ 17. "using Resuci-Annie."
   _____ 18. "without noticeable discomfort."
   _____ 19. "identify anatomical parts."
   _____ 20. "before dismantling the fuel line . . ."

3. Classify each of the abbreviated performance objectives found below as: **(A)** affective domain, **(C)** cognitive domain, or **(P)** psychomotor domain.

   _____ 1. Given 25 specific situations and two alternative solutions for each, the student will determine which of the two possible solutions to each problem of union unrest is most likely to eliminate the problem.

_____   2. The student will be able to recite the decimal equivalents of common fractional measurements with no more than two errors.

_____   3. The student will be able to properly load the cartridge so that when the device is turned on, the ribbon will be taut and in place.

_____   4. The student will demonstrate an interest in conservation by attending eight out of ten presentations offered during the year by the Outdoors Club.

_____   5. Given descriptions of ten construction projects requiring slabs, the student will calculate the quantity of concrete needed for each within a tolerance of ¼ cubic yard.

_____   6. The student will demonstrate concern for the democratic principles of free enterprise by articulating at least one principle verbally during an ungraded class discussion.

_____   7. The student will show a growing awareness of health occupations by participating at least twice in health club discussions.

_____   8. The student will be able to transfer bacteria from a culture to a petri dish in a manner which produces properly spread colonies. No contamination is permitted.

_____   9. The student will show interest in industrial occupations by associating the names of at least 15 job titles out of 20 with their job tasks in an ungraded, optional exercise inventory.

_____   10. After reading an article on small engine performance, the student will summarize the article in no more than 100 words.

_____   11. The student will be able to drill a hole in tool steel using a carbide tip drill within .01 of an inch.

_____   12. The student will name the symbols on an electrical schematic drawing with 80% accuracy.

_____   13. Given three situations requiring correspondence, the student will compose, type, and print a business letter for each, taking no longer than 25 minutes per letter.

_____   14. After watching a rehearsed machining demonstration, the student will be able to criticize in writing at least three safety rules that were violated during the operations.

_____   15. The student will show appreciation and enjoyment in the foods lab by willingly helping to return equipment to its proper place at least three times per week.

_____   16. The students will be able to administer an intramuscular injection using the proper technique.

_____   17. By the end of the second week of instruction, when given standard patterns, all students will be able to compute the amount of fabric needed to within ½ yard of material.

_____   18. All student nurses will demonstrate a positive attitude toward their duties as a technologist by willingly seeking out activities that will help polish their skills.

_____   19. The student will be able to read 10 different settings on a goniometer within 10 minutes and with no more than plus or minus 2 degrees of error.

_____   20. Given the necessary instruments, the student will be able to measure supination and pronation on a peer to acceptable clinical standards.

4. Write one performance objective for your instructional program in each of the three learning domains. Use the checklist provided to make sure that the objective is complete.

    a. *Cognitive Domain*

    _____ Performance Objective: _____

    _____

    _____

    _____

    Checklist: Who ____ Does What ____ Under What Conditions ____
    How Well ____ In What Time ____ Measured By ____

    b. *Affective Domain*

    _____ Performance Objective: _____

    _____

    _____

    _____

    Checklist: Who ____ Does What ____ Under What Conditions ____
    How Well ____ In What Time ____ Measured By ____

    c. *Psychomotor Domain*

    _____ Performance Objective: _____

    _____

    _____

    _____

    Checklist: Who ____ Does What ____ Under What Conditions ____
    How Well ____ In What Time ____ Measured By ____

5. Select one unit of instruction from the course or program that you teach or are preparing to teach and prepare ten performance objectives for each of the three learning domains. All objectives should be written in such a format that they provide answers to the questions: who, does what, under what conditions, in what time, how well, as measured by. Group your objectives according to the learning domain.

6. Using the Instructor's Lesson Plan that was described in this chapter as a guide, prepare a lesson plan for at least one lesson that you give (or will give) in your course. It is suggested that you prepare this first lesson plan for one of your introductory lessons that is at least one hour in length. Once you use this form, you may wish to adapt it to more specifically fit your needs.

6 There's More Than One Way to Skin a Cat

Techniques of Teaching

THE INSTRUCTIONAL PROCESS involves, more than anything else, the communication of information, thoughts, and ideas. There is always more than one way to skin a cat, there is more than one way to communicate (or teach) the subject matter of occupational education. The method used is largely determined by the results of the job and task analyses and the objectives sought. Teaching is communication, whether we use a lecture, a demonstration, or any other method. For that reason, this chapter, which is devoted to descriptions of the most common instructional methods, begins with a section on communication skills.

Communication Skills

Teachers are always communicators, and they are speakers much of the time. Skill in communicating is essential for success as a teacher. An understanding of the significant relationships between the basic elements of the communicative process can help you improve your ability to communicate effectively. As a teacher, you speak primarily to impart new knowledge or to clarify what the students already know.

No matter how well the subject matter is known and how well instructional materials have been planned, organized, and supported, the real test of teaching is the student behavior that results from the presentation. Skillful use of the voice with appropriate body action is essential to the effective presentation of subject content.

Definition

Communication might be defined as the transmission of feelings, ideas, facts, and attitudes from one mind to another. The effectiveness of communication is measured by the similarity between the ideas transmitted and the ideas received.

Elements of Communication

The process of communication is comprised of the interaction of three basic elements: the *communicator* (teacher), the *symbols* used in transmitting the message (words, pictures, images), and the *receiver* (student).

Communicator. The effectiveness of the communicator is influenced by (1) the ability to select and use language or symbols that are meaningful to the students; (2) the attitudes of the communicators toward themselves, the subject, and the receivers; and (3) the wealth of current, accurate, and stimulating information available. In other words, teachers must know how to use the language; they must love themselves, the subject, and the students; and they need to know what they are talking about.

Symbols.   The second element of the communication process is the symbolic, or the oral and visual, code used to transmit information. The letters of the alphabet arranged as words are a basic code. Gestures such as waving and facial expressions are forms of basic visual codes or symbols. Ideas are communicated only when symbols are combined in meaningful wholes. Thus, words are selected to form sentences, and related sentences are combined to form paragraphs. Each part of the whole is important for effective communication.

Receiver.   The third element of communication is the receiver. A basic rule of thumb might be that communication succeeds only in relation to the reaction of the receiver. If the receiver does not fully understand, or worse—misunderstands—there is usually some sort of signal to the communicator indicating the need for clarification until the desired behavior change is accomplished. It is very important for the communicator to be on the alert for these signals and to adjust a presentation accordingly. When the receiver (student) reacts with understanding and their behavior changes to indicate their understanding, then communication has taken place. Remember, students all bring different abilities, attitudes, and experiences to class, so a wide range of signals might be sent during one presentation—each of them meaning something different, and the teacher is required to decode all of them.

Communication Techniques

Since the teacher is the source of information being transmitted, it stands to reason that the teacher is the most important element in the classroom communication process. Language, mannerisms, body language, and eye contact all play major roles in effective communication.

Language

Perhaps the greatest single barrier to effective communication in the classroom is the lack of a common core of experience between the teacher and the students. Communication can be effective only to the extent that the experiences of the persons concerned are similar. This lack of a common core is most pronounced in vocabulary and language use.

Most occupational education is of a technical nature—teachers refer to objects, machines, and processes using the language of the workplace. Unless the students have had some experience with the objects or concepts discussed, the words used will be meaningless or misinterpreted.

At the beginning of instruction and until all students have a basic understanding of all technical terms, words and phrases should be chosen with the students' backgrounds in mind, thereby establishing a common core or experience that is basic to effective communication.

The type of words to use to describe concrete or abstract ideas is most important for effective communication. Consider the declaration, "I bought a dog."

The mental image each person forms will vary because there are so many different kinds of dogs. "I bought a two-year old German Shepard," creates a mental image that corresponds to the idea intended. Nearly everyone knows what a full-grown German Shepard looks like, so the statement is understood because the listeners can relate it to their direct experience.

On the other hand, abstract words represent ideas that cannot be directly perceived, or ideas that may not produce mental images in the receiver's mind. Abstract words usually can be related to more than one interpretation by the reader or listener. The abstraction *professional* cannot be directly experienced by most beginning occupational education students. But after a period of instruction and observation on the job, *professional* comes to have some meaning. Abstract words are necessary and useful, for they serve as shorthand symbols that sum up vast areas of experience.

If we were forced to use only concrete words, we would soon bog down in detail, so it becomes necessary to use abstract words for their convenience. It is important to remember when using abstractions to link them with specific experiences through examples and illustrations. Even better, reduce the level of abstraction by using concrete and specific words as much as possible. By using concrete words, you will narrow and gain better control of the images produced in the minds of the students.

Voice Control

The qualities of a teacher's voice significantly influences how students receive and react to what is said. Your voice conveys sincerity or insincerity, enthusiasm or boredom, self-confidence or fear, and other attitudes and personality traits. Pitch, rate, force, and clarity are the four characteristics affecting voice quality and subsequently the quality of communication.

Vocal *pitch* refers to the highness or lowness of the sound of the voice. When we say that a singer has a high voice, or a deep voice, we are describing pitch. Varying the pitch of your voice prevents speaking in a monotone and will make your voice more pleasant to the students.

Rate refers to the speed of talking. Maintaining a constant rate will cause your students to become bored and to focus their attention on something other than what you are saying. Sometimes you know you are speaking too rapidly or too slowly by the facial expressions of your students. Often a student will ask you to repeat something "a little more slowly." When presenting difficult material or emphasizing a point, speaking at a slower-than-usual rate is appropriate.

If all students cannot hear you or if you "drown them out," then the *force* or volume of your voice is not appropriate. The size of the room, number of students, your distance from the students, and the level of background noise are some of the factors that will determine how loud you should talk. Adjust your volume to the conditions so that everyone can hear you.

Clarity in speech is characterized by speaking distinctly and by avoiding verbal mannerisms. If you slur your words or speak out of the sides of your mouth, your listeners cannot accurately receive and interpret what you say. Your students may have difficulty understanding you if you use no more lung power and lip movements than you do when talking with one person. If you lack self-confidence in knowledge of the subject or are nervous speaking to a group, your speech may be muffled or hesitant.

Verbal mannerisms are the distracting use of words, phrases, or sounds. We all know how distracting it is to listen to someone who starts every sentence with "uhh," frequently clears the throat or sniffs through the nose, and then finishes the sentence with "you know" or "If you know what I mean." You may not be aware of such mannerisms in your delivery unless you listen to your voice on tape or receive an honest critique. When you learn about it, make a conscientious and determined effort to avoid such behavior.

A good speaking voice is pleasant, free from distracting or unpleasant characteristics, easily heard, and characterized by variety in pitch, rate, and force. Concentrate on improving these qualities every time you make a presentation.

Bodily Actions

Gestures, movement from one place to another, facial expressions, and posture are bodily actions that enhance or detract from your communication ability. When these actions result from a genuine desire to communicate they will serve to complement, reinforce, and clarify what you say with your voice. Bodily actions, like the voice, also reflect attitudes and feelings.

Effective teachers use their entire body to communicate instruction. If you are thoroughly prepared for each teaching assignment and are sincerely interested in the subject matter, your bodily actions will convey this self-confidence, enthusiasm, and sincerity to the students.

Good teachers do not rely on rules for gesturing and moving. Rather, these actions occur spontaneously as reactions to a genuine impulse to clarify or emphasize the subject content. Gestures and movements that are deliberately used for their own sake usually do not convince the students and may actually detract from what is spoken. As you gain confidence in speaking to a group, your gestures and movements will become more natural, thus aiding you in communicating with your students.

Your feelings and attitudes toward the subject, the students, and yourself are conveyed to the students by your facial expressions and posture. Whether you are bored, confused, tense, relaxed, or enthusiastic, you will unintentionally show these feelings by the way you stand or move and the expression on your face. You might use gestures and words that indicate confidence and enthusiasm, but slumped shoulders and a deadpan expression will convey your real feelings.

Pacing, coin jingling, head scratching, chalk juggling, pointer tapping, and pen clicking are but a few of the actions that can draw attention away from what you are saying. These physical mannerisms, like vocal mannerisms, are usually a means of relieving tension. You can break these habits if you become aware that you have them and that they are distracting.

Eye Contact

Some teachers seem to address the ceiling, a spot on the floor, or some object outside a window rather than their students. This failure to look students in the eye usually indicates some fear, timidity, or embarrassment. Lack of direct eye contact with your students will give them the impression that you lack interest in the subject and in them. Direct eye contact will give the students the feeling that you are talking *with* them, not simply *at* or in front of them.

Direct eye contact will also help you spot difficulties by checking for signs of doubt, disagreement, confusion, boredom, and other reactions. This provides the feedback for adjustments in your presentation in order to regain the students' attention and confidence.

Summary

An understanding of the communication process helps the teacher to communicate effectively. The three basic elements, the communicator, the symbols, and the receiver, are dynamically interrelated. The teacher must reduce the barriers to communication by establishing or determining a common core of experience. Abstractions should be clarified through examples, comparisons, and illustrations.

An effective teacher has a speaking voice that is pleasant, easily heard, and free from distracting, unpleasant characteristics. Distinctive speech with variations in pitch, rate, and force will produce emphasis and promote student learning. Speech is complemented, reinforced, and clarified by gestures and other spontaneous, appropriate body actions. Feelings and attitudes are reflected through facial expressions and posture. Direct eye contact with students indicates interest in them as individuals and serves as a method of obtaining feedback on the presentation.

Instructional Techniques

Most methods and techniques of instruction can be described by one or more of the simple words: telling, discussing, showing, and doing. The instructional techniques that are discussed in the following paragraphs are combinations of these. The most appropriate method used to teach a particular lesson or class is *not* determined by the teacher's preference. Instead, the most appropriate method is determined by the objectives of the course or lesson.

Remember that in occupational education, every method requires activity (doing something) by the student. You will recall that this principle is most easily recognized when the learning is directed toward the acquisition of a physical skill, but it is no less true of mental or cognitive effort. A student's effort to understand, to organize, to follow a thought, to solve a problem, or to memorize facts is "doing" just as much as when practicing a manipulative skill. In fact, even in the case of manipulative skills, mental *doing* is often of equal or more importance than the physical *doing* because the mind keeps track of the proper sequence of steps, can be alert to key points in the performance of the skill, and can seek out ways of perfecting the physical portion of the skill. Think back for a moment of the time when you learned a particularly difficult skill or procedure. How much practice did you get just by performing the skill over and over in your mind? Recent research in brain activity has shown that the same areas of the brain are active when one thinks about performing something as when they are actually performing the act. It is believed that we *exercise* the skill and thereby reinforce the learning just by mentally practicing it! You might not want to share this information with your students, or the next time they are just sitting around instead of working in the lab they will tell you that they are mentally practicing. In any case, the importance of practice cannot be overstated.

The Lecture Method

Most oral presentations are called lectures and may take several forms and have various purposes. The *illustrated talk* in which the speaker relies heavily on visual aids to convey ideas to the listeners is one form of lecture. Teachers on educational television, for example, are bound by the medium to giving illustrated talks.

Another form of lecture is the *briefing*, wherein the speaker presents a concise array of facts to the listeners who do not expect elaboration or supporting material. Superintendents of schools often deliver briefings to the staff at the beginning of a school year.

The third type of lecture, rarely used in education, is the *formal speech* in which the speaker's purpose is to inform, to persuade, or to entertain. Essayists, poets, and secretaries of state deliver speeches.

The *teaching lecture* for which the teacher must plan and deliver an oral presentation in a manner that helps the students reach the desired learning outcomes is the fourth type of lecture. Lecturing is one of the oldest, most used, and most useful methods of teaching. It is also the method that has the most potential for misuse. You may have heard the saying "telling isn't teaching." One joker took it a little further and said that a lecture is "the transfer of information from the teacher's notes to the students' notebooks without passing through the mind of either." Such comments do not have to be true.

Teaching lectures are generally of two types: formal and informal. The *formal lecture* is primarily used when presenting information to large groups. Communication is virtually a one-way flow from the teacher to the students. Student participation is severely limited and essentially passive. The formal lecture is used extensively in large university classes such as in biology, which is later broken into smaller lab classes. The presentation of a common base of information to all students is assured by using this method, but if students have immediate questions or need for feedback, they are not likely to get it in this class.

In the *informal lecture*, the teacher creates activity by (1) encouraging the students to ask questions if they do not understand, and (2) asking the students questions to determine their progress. The informal lecture method incorporates the principles of learning and teaching regarding student involvement that were discussed in earlier chapters.

Advantages and Disadvantages.   The advantages of using the lecture method include: (1) saving time, (2) saving person-power, and (3) supplementing other teaching methods. By using this method the teacher can present many ideas in a relatively short time. Information that either might require extensive research by students or is not available in reference material can be quickly presented. In addition, lessons that are suitable for lectures can be presented to large groups of students by one person. Budget-minded administrators like this! Finally, the lecture method can and usually *must* be used to supplement discussions and demonstrations. It is difficult to imagine any other method being used to introduce and summarize most lessons.

The lecture method does have its limitations. First, even with the informal method, it limits student participation. Second, the lecture method is not suitable for teaching students skills such as typing, adjusting a machine, or manipulating tools. The third disadvantage is that the teacher has difficulty accurately evaluating student progress. Finally, many teachers find it difficult to keep student attention and interest at a high level during a lecture.

Some techniques for maximizing the advantages and minimizing the disadvantages of the lecture are discussed in the following paragraphs.

Lecture Techniques.   The informal teaching lecture is probably most effective when delivered in an extemporaneous manner using an outline. The teacher speaks from a written outline but does not read or memorize the material to be presented. The exact words with which to express an idea are left to the moment, so the lecture is more personalized than one that is read or spoken from memory. Since the teacher speaks directly to the students, their reactions can be readily observed, and adjustments can be made to their responses. For example, if puzzled expressions indicate that a number of students fail to grasp an idea, that point can be elaborated upon until the reactions or responses to questions indicate that they understand.

The extemporaneous, informal lecture reflects the teacher's personal enthusiasm and is more flexible than the formal lecture. For these reasons, it is likely to hold the interest of the students.

The effective informal lecture includes the use of techniques such as (1) verbal support material, (2) visual aids, (3) emphasis of key points, (4) student interaction, and (5) effective speech delivery.

Verbal support material includes stories or anecdotes that support a point made and that make the lesson more interesting, more understandable, and therefore, easier for the students. Relating personal experiences, asides about well-known persons, or incidents that occur on the job serve as verbal support material.

Visual aids can be used to help clarify and illustrate ideas. Students encounter difficulties in making verbal descriptions meaningful, especially in technical material. Maps, sketches, diagrams, and models, along with the words of description are very effective. The use of charts, graphs, pictures, and slides not only reinforce explanations, but they also decrease the necessary explanation time and increase the students' understanding.

Instruction will not be effective unless the important parts of the lesson have been emphasized so that they stand out. Often it is effective to say "This point is very important" in order to add emphasis. Underlining words on the board or the overhead transparency adds emphasis and requires the students to think through and comprehend ideas as they are presented.

The teacher can achieve active student interaction in the informal lecture through the use of questions. In this way students are encouraged to make contributions to supplement the lecture. Questions can be used for one or more of the following purposes: to determine the experience and background of the students in order to tailor the lecture to their needs, to add variety and stimulate interest, and to check student understanding. Because it is used in so many of the instructional methods, a separate section on questioning techniques is included later in this chapter.

An effective speech delivery is the real test of the lecture. If the presentation lacks force, effectiveness, and dignity, the ideas will not be clarified and the objectives will not be met. To communicate effectively, the teacher must be heard, use voice variation, use appropriate gestures, maintain eye contact, and avoid distracting mannerisms. The success of the lecture is directly related to the skill, knowledge, and enthusiasm of the lecturer.

The Guided Discussion Method

The discussion method of teaching is essentially an interchange of ideas and knowledge by the students under the guidance of the teacher. For most people, discussion is a common part of everyday living. Friends and co-workers discuss world events over coffee and lunch. Families discuss world events, common interests, worries, and joys. Some even discuss religion and politics! Quite often during discussions our thoughts and attitudes toward the subject change or take shape. Because discussion is a familiar way of exchanging ideas and developing firm conclusions, it is ideally suited for some classroom use.

The guided discussion may be defined as a method of teaching in which the teacher uses questions to cause students to actively participate in the learning situation by exchanging ideas, opinions, and experiences in order to reach conclusions that will support course objectives. Speaking of objectives—the discussion method is best suited to those objectives that demand the development of understanding and reasoning rather than manipulative skills. Cognitive knowledge such as facts and figures may be reinforced by repetition during discussion, but the method is best used to develop skill in the higher levels of the cognitive domain and in all levels of the affective domain. (Refer to Chapter 5 for a review of the three domains of learning.)

Advantages and Disadvantages.   The guided discussion method has many advantages for both the teacher and the students. A well-planned and guided discussion provides for active student participation. Don't forget that learning increases and is strengthened by active participation. A discussion provides each student with a greater opportunity to respond individually to the lesson objectives. Students are called upon to present their own views, answers, or solutions to the group. The others mentally participate by judging the validity of what is being said.

The discussion method stimulates effective thinking because students have to think reflectively. One school of thought in education views learning as problem solving . . . that life and work constitute a series of problems, all of which are more or less serious. Solution of these problems is the key to survival. The Harvard Business School uses a form of guided discussion, the case study method, for virtually all instruction.

When using the discussion method, students' misconceptions can be corrected. As the discussion progresses, other students often will explain what is correct and why, thereby reinforcing their own learning as well.

Contrary to the cartoons that we see about objects designed by committees, groups seem to arrive at better solutions to problems than individuals do. In contributing to these group solutions, all students feel that they are part of a team effort and when they arrive at a logical conclusion they have achieved the lesson objectives. Discussion, then, becomes a way to promote class spirit.

There are disadvantages or limitations on the use of the guided discussion method. Even with the best planning and guidance by the teacher, discussions take more time than lectures. With all students participating, it is difficult to keep the discussion on track.

Many discussions fail or take too long because the teacher does not ask the correct questions to lead students to the core of the issue. The teacher employing this method has to have a good command of questioning techniques.

The advantage of active student participation is lost if there are more than 15 to 20 students in a discussion group. A good informal exchange of ideas can quickly turn into a contest to be heard if too many people attempt to participate, so discussions should be used in smaller groups when possible.

Finally, discussion participants need to have sufficient background and knowledge so they can talk about the subject. Discussions are often used in occupational education to develop abstract concepts such as the work ethic, responsibility, and employee or employer rights. For technical material, students must have enough knowledge to make the discussion worthwhile. If all class members do not understand the fundamentals of the subject, the discussion is likely to be dominated by a few students, or worse, the entire class will be unable to discuss the topic at all.

Below are some techniques for using the guided discussion method.

Discussion Techniques.   Conducting an effective discussion requires thorough preparation on the part of the teacher and the students. The selection of a topic that students can profitably discuss is based on the course objectives. Those objectives that state or imply an "understanding" or "feeling" level of learning are prime candidates for discussion topics. A specific objective should be established for the discussion.

Once the lesson objective is established, it is necessary to conduct enough research to become familiar with all facets of the discussion topic. This is an ideal time to prepare and assign background homework for the students.

A guided discussion has three main parts—an introduction, the discussion itself, and a conclusion. Evaluation of student learning is continuous as the teacher observes and guides the discussion. In planning a discussion, the teacher's job is to be sure that discussion points are arranged to logically reach the objective.

If a number of factual points or learning objectives are desired, a lead-off question should be prepared for each one. Lead-off questions should begin with *how* or *why,* since the purpose is to bring about discussion rather than merely to get answers.

When all parties are prepared, a guided discussion begins with an *introduction* in the same manner as a lecture or any other teaching method. The introduction should include attention and motivation steps and an overview of key points.

The *discussion* itself is then opened by asking one of the prepared lead-off questions. The students should then be given a few moments to react, for unlike the teacher, they do not have an answer readily at hand. It is wise to begin with an easy question because the more difficult the question, the more time will be needed to produce an answer.

Once one or two questions are answered, the discussion is usually well underway. As the discussion proceeds, it is often necessary to guide the direction by using *how* and *why* follow-up questions. Students will often anticipate the discussion guide's questions and ask them of other students.

When it appears that the ideas supporting a particular point have been discussed, the teacher should provide a summary of what has been discussed. This *interim summary* brings the ideas together and aids in the transition to the next learning point. Interim summaries should be made after each point. It is desirable to record ideas, facts, and agreements as the discussion progresses so that the students can see the relationships that have been made.

A guided discussion is closed by *summarizing* the material that has been covered. Loose ends are related to main points and a conclusion is reached. For example, in concluding a discussion on the work ethic, a teacher might describe a person who has achieved success on the job and why.

Although evaluation in the form of teacher observation is an integral part of the discussion, the teacher should check again to determine if all students understand the material. In particular, questions should be directed to class members who were less active during the discussion. If students are not able to answer the check questions, the topic should be summarized and briefly retaught.

One final point is crucial to the successful discussion: the classroom atmosphere. The typical teacher-in-the-front, students-in-rows arrangement is not conducive to a give-and-take discussion. Seats should be arranged in a circle (best), semi-circle (excellent), hollow square (good), or U-shaped configuration. It is important that all participants have a direct line of sight to other participants, including the teacher. This will produce a more relaxed atmosphere and help to draw the timid students into the discussion.

Summary.   Guided discussion is a method of teaching in which questions are used to cause students to actively participate in the learning situation. Discussions are useful for stimulating reflective thinking, promoting class spirit, and identifying and correcting misconceptions. Discussions are time-consuming and are limited by class size, knowledge, and experience.

Effective techniques for use in guiding discussions include the use of lead-off and follow-up questions and an appropriate, open seating arrangement. A nonthreatening atmosphere should be created and all students drawn into the discussion. Interim summaries help to keep the discussion on track, and a final summary and conclusion will reinforce what has been learned.

Teaching by Demonstration

The lecture and discussion methods are used to teach facts, theory, and principles. The demonstration method consists of displaying equipment and instruments or showing correct procedures and processes. It may constitute a lesson in itself, but it is usually only part of a lesson, the last half consisting of actual performance by the students. The performance component will be discussed in the next section.

Demonstrations require careful planning and practice before they are given since they exemplify the teacher's skill and that which is expected of the students. The demonstration, coupled with student performance, is the basic technique for teaching and learning manipulative skills.

Advantages and Disadvantages.   The use of the demonstration method makes explanations concrete by showing what is being said. The students see the skill being performed and hear the explanation at the same time, thereby relating the theory and facts they have learned to a practical situation.

Also, the demonstration method appeals to more than one sense. It allows the student to not only hear what is being done, but to see it as well.

A correctly performed demonstration will reduce student performance errors. Students will attempt to imitate the teacher, using the methods and techniques demonstrated.

There are two distinct disadvantages to the demonstration method. First, it demands a greater degree of skill on the teacher's part than just being able to perform the task. At times demonstrations must be performed from abnormal or unusual positions, such as standing behind and above the equipment or process. In addition, while the skill is being performed, the teacher has to explain each step in the process along with all necessary safety precautions.

Finally, since the students do not perform during the demonstration, it is difficult to evaluate their learning. This disadvantage can be minimized through questioning while the demonstration is being performed.

Techniques.   To get the maximum benefit from a demonstration, use the actual tools, materials, and equipment whenever possible. The students get to see the skill performed on the actual equipment they will use on the job. This makes the learning more realistic. If the actual equipment is not available or is impractical to use in an instructional situation, models or mock-ups can be used. Instructional aids are essential for maximum student learning when using the demonstration method.

Practice the demonstration to ensure correct performance. Nothing is more confusing for the students, or frustrating for the teacher, than to have a demonstration not work properly. Assemble all the necessary equipment, tools, materials, and instructional aids in sufficient time prior to class for a pre-check and to be sure everything is in working order. This step is easy, of course, because you have included all the needed items on your Instructor's Lesson Plan.

Before starting a demonstration, it is necessary to motivate the students and to get them *ready* to learn. Do this by instructing them to pay attention and to ask questions if they are confused or to answer questions or perform if called upon. Be sure that the students know exactly what the objective of the lesson is.

Position the students and the instructional aid or equipment so that all students can see the operation, preferably from the direction in which they will perform it. Do not start until all students are situated properly to see the demonstration.

Begin the demonstration by showing and explaining the operations in a step-by-step order. Whenever possible, the telling and doing should be done simultaneously. Speed of performance should not be emphasized in the demonstration. Make certain that the students understand the first step before proceeding to the second, and so on. Difficult operations should be repeated. It helps to pause briefly after each operation to check student comprehension by questioning them.

During the demonstration, always observe safety precautions. It takes a few more seconds to don safety glasses or other protective clothing, but the time is not wasted. The students are being impressed with the importance of exercising care in dealing with potentially dangerous equipment or substances.

The students learn facts and associate parts of the process during a demonstration, so it is important to give proper attention to terminology. Just mentioning the names of parts is usually not enough. Students might be referred to a chalkboard or chart where all the correct nomenclature can be found. It also helps to conduct a terminology drill on the parts of the demonstration aid while it is in its assembled or disassembled condition, as appropriate.

Watch the class during the demonstration for reactions indicating lack of attention, confusion, or doubt, but do not depend entirely on visual observations. Ask questions that require the students to recall nomenclature, procedural steps, underlying principles, and safety precautions.

Depending on the complexity of the skill, there is generally a need for the inclusion of one or more repetitions of the demonstration. The more complex the skill, the greater the need for repetition. The job should be repeated at least once without noticeable interruptions, other than a restatement of the procedure and the safety precautions. This repetition should be performed with the proper, or normal, degree of ease, speed, and accuracy. The standard of speed is usually that which the majority of students will be expected to attain.

At the conclusion of the demonstration, check for comprehension again by questioning the students. This is also an ideal time to invite students to ask questions regarding the process or procedure.

Summary.   The demonstration method is the teaching method by which the teacher explains and shows the students the precise actions necessary to perform skills or processes. It makes explanations concrete, appeals to more than one sense, sets a standard for student performance, and helps make student performance safer. The demonstration is an incomplete process for teaching a skill and must be used in conjunction with practical exercises or student performance.

The body of the demonstration lesson plan must contain an introduction that motivates the students to learn, a step-by-step breakdown of the process, key points to be remembered, safety precautions, and sample questions to ask the students to check their comprehension. The safety of students and equipment must be assured at all times during the demonstration.

The Performance Method

The performance method, which is also commonly called the practical exercise method, allows students the opportunity to practice, perform, and apply—under controlled conditions and close supervision—the skills or processes that have been explained and demonstrated.

Some skills (welding, equipment repair, cosmetology, carpentry) culminate in a finished product or service. For such skills, performance consists mainly of practice making the product or performing the service until the required standards of ease and precision are reached. For other skills, such as typing, the important of practice is mainly on the development of speed and accuracy.

Advantages and Disadvantages.   The advantages of using the student performance method are that it provides for individual guidance and evaluation of student activity and that it permits the students to apply principles and theories to practice. Learning is reinforced through application.

Conversely, the method is time-consuming because students must be provided the opportunity to practice until they reach a specific degree of proficiency. Special rooms or laboratories may be required to store equipment and student projects. The equipment required for student performance may be expensive and require constant preventative maintenance and scheduled periodic maintenance by qualified personnel. The performance method usually requires a higher teacher to student ratio than the other methods of instruction.

Techniques.   Skill development should be planned to progress from the simple to the complex. To keep the students from having to memorize the steps in the process, provide specific detailed instructions for them to follow when practicing the skill. These instructions are called procedure sheets and should be reproduced in sufficient quantity for all students to have one at their practice station.

Set up realistic work problems. The students gain a sense of accomplishment when they solve or complete problems that they will encounter on the job. Make-work or busy-work problems that are not used in an actual work situation will usually bore the students, will not be taken seriously, and will not provide them with skills necessary for survival on the job.

While the students are performing, ask appropriate questions to make sure that they understand what they are doing and to ensure that they are practicing safety. Questions should be asked during short pauses in the practice. Avoid interrupting students while they are working or their concentration might be broken. Even if the students pause or are hesitant, leave them alone if they are correctly performing the process. But do not hesitate to interrupt if you see students making or about to make mistakes. Assist students in ways that help them work independently. Do not take over the project unless it is absolutely necessary to re-demonstrate part of the skill or to ensure safety.

While the students are performing, evaluate their procedures as well as the end product. The students should be required to use the steps and procedures taught in the demonstration. The demonstration should have set the standard for attainment, so evaluate performance in terms of time, quantity, and quality.

Summary.   The performance method provides the students opportunity to practice, perform, and apply the skills or processes taught in the demonstration. Through these practical exercises, the students acquire the necessary skills they will use on the job. Practice reinforces learning because students apply principles and theories to realistic situations.

The effectiveness of the performance method is increased by using realistic work projects, observing student behavior during performance, assisting students when necessary, and evaluating their procedures and end product. A lesson plan for the performance method should contain a standard motivating introduction, instructions for initiating student performance, work area assignments, and procedures for evaluating student work.

A Potpourri of Methods

The four methods of instruction most common to classroom-based occupational education have been discussed on the preceding pages. The demonstration and student performance methods are often combined for one lesson or procedure. There are many other methods of instruction. A detailed discussion of all of them is beyond the scope of this book, but a brief description of the most common of these methods follows. (Consult the bibliography at the end of this chapter for more in-depth descriptions of those methods.)

Individualized Instruction. This method refers to time during which students obtain information via a workbook, a programmed text, videotape, CD-ROM, a regular text, directly from the teacher, or from any other source of information. Individualized units are not normally used for an entire class or course, but they could be. Research studies have revealed that individualized instruction, if properly planned and executed, not only conserves teacher time for more valuable and personal help to students but also produces as high a quality of learning as the teacher-controlled methods. Some methods or techniques closely related to or used with individualized instruction include self-directed learning, self-paced modules, mentoring, tutoring, contract instruction, and workshops. The reader is encouraged to consult the bibliography at the end of the chapter for help in using these valuable techniques.

Variations of the Discussion Method. Several variations of the guided discussion may be used to teach attitudes and facts. The *conference* is very similar to the guided discussion, except that teachers present facts that they wish students to learn. The students then develop the knowledge through individual questions that develop the ideas that the teacher wishes to teach. The conference method is used when the teacher is sure that the ideas presented will be accepted by the students as true.

Another variation of the discussion is the *case study*. In this method a problem is presented by the teacher for consideration, discussion, and possible solution. The case consists of a statement of facts, opinions, and problems (real or hypothetical) that must be faced and solved. The case study method is helpful in teaching some general subjects, leadership, and work management fundamentals.

A *seminar* consists of a group of supervised students who present their individual problems, findings, or opinions in order to receive the benefit of constructive criticism or advice from their peers. The teacher serves as a moderator and resource person.

Another form of discussion is the *panel* or committee, where an orderly and logical presentation of material is made to the class by several people having some special knowledge of the subject. Panel discussions are often used to present divergent points of view. Panel participants must be carefully selected and briefed in advance. The teacher usually introduces the topic and the panelists, asks key questions to start the discussion, guides it, and summarizes it.

Programmed Instruction. Programmed instruction is a method of instruction wherein each student can progress at individual speed toward a definite and preestablished objective. The *program,* or bits of information, is usually provided by means of a machine (often a computer) or a programmed textbook. As students progress through instructional materials, they make a response to each increment of instruction. The material offers them immediate feedback by informing them of the correctness of their responses. The successful completion of each increment takes the students one step closer to the planned objective.

Material presented as programmed instruction is also commonly known as computer-managed instruction or computer-assisted instruction. Great strides have been made with this method, especially with the advent of multimedia computers. Programmed instruction is best suited for use in teaching cognitive skills or facts, ideas, and concepts. It is difficult to teach students attitudes or values using programmed instruction and nearly impossible to teach manipulative skills.

Cooperative Learning.   Another method of instruction, or rather a teaching and learning technique or strategy, has emerged from the idea of cooperative learning. Cooperative learning helps students develop skills such as working and cooperating with other individuals and groups (interdependence), team-building, and other social interaction skills that will facilitate the students' transition from the classroom to the workplace. Using cooperative learning strategies in the classroom comes easily only to teachers who firmly believe in the technique, so it is important that one learns the method before trying it the first time. Several excellent references may be found at the end of the chapter.

Summary.   There are many methods of instruction in addition to the lecture, the discussion, and the demonstration-performance. Most of these methods are limited to the presentation of isolated types of knowledge or special skills. All teaching or learning methods require careful planning by the teacher, careful execution, and appropriate practice for the students. A complete lesson plan is used for all types of lessons in order to focus the topic and to ensure more effective learning.

Questions in Instruction

The teacher's skill in questioning is an important contribution to student learning in all methods of instruction. The question is one of the most effective teaching devices, having a variety of uses and value with almost any teaching method. The teacher who knows how to skillfully use questions is seldom a poor teacher. It does take time to develop and practice the ability to ask the right question of the right student at the right time, but the time and effort is well spent. The ability to question is one of the teacher's most valuable tricks of the trade.

Some teachers (even experienced ones) have the misconception that questions are used only in the discussion method of instruction. In fact, the demonstration method lends itself very well to the questioning technique, as questions can be asked on key points, nomenclature, and safety precautions. Quite often during informal lectures, teachers will ask questions to help students tie the lecture together and to serve as a transition to the next major point.

In order for learning to take place, there has to be two-way communication in the classroom. Questions are one way of achieving this two-way communication. Questions serve several purposes, and the purpose will determine how each question should be asked.

Purposes of Questioning

From the time that people learn to ask *Why?* we constantly ask questions to learn and answer questions that others ask of us. There are many purposes for questions and questioning, but we will discuss the seven most common purposes here.

Some teachers ask a question of the class before they begin a lecture. This is an example of a question used to *get and maintain interest*. Discussions are often opened with a lead-off question that has the purpose of focusing attention and getting the discussion started. A good question will get the students' attention immediately. The answer, which is in the teacher's mind, should be within all the students' realms of knowledge. If their answers are close enough, go to the next question or use it to move into the lecture.

Questions that are properly planned and phrased will *stimulate students* to think for themselves. The "proper planning" includes establishing a permissive atmosphere where students feel free to answer. You will recall that students have a lot to lose in terms of their self-esteem, so an atmosphere where there is no *dumb* question will allow them to answer or give their personal opinion without fear of failure.

Use of questions can give you a chance to *evaluate and summarize* your teaching. The questions should evaluate and check understanding of the lesson objectives. This allows for the immediate correction of misconceptions or faulty information.

Once an informal lecture or a discussion is underway, questions are used to keep the class alive and to *distribute opportunity* for class participation among students. The teacher's questions, directed toward specific students, will keep one or two students from dominating the class.

Proper distribution of questions will encourage individual students to take advantage of the group's skill and experience by *participating* in it. A class in which all students participate tends to be more tolerant, and members will not be afraid to express divergent views.

Questions are a good method of *determining student attitudes*. Enthusiastic participation in a class discussion depends on the manner in which students are included in the lesson. Negative attitudes may be overcome and changed by the deft use of questions.

The final purpose of questioning is to *develop the subject*. Questions that develop the subject are those that logically lead the students from the known to the unknown and from the simple to the complex.

Characteristics of Questions

A good question has a purpose, it is clear and concise, it is related to the objectives, it is challenging, and it is limited to one idea.

A purposeful question is asked specifically to obtain student attention, open or stimulate discussion, discover weaknesses, change the direction of a discussion, distribute class participation, check understanding, or to stimulate interest.

There are many more reasons for asking questions, but the purpose should be clear in the teacher's mind. Why take up valuable time to ask a question not related to the lesson objectives?

Students must know exactly what is being asked in order to give a correct answer. A clear question, worded in terms understood by the students, will give them the same mental picture that is intended.

Questions should be related to the lesson objectives. Little benefit will be derived if the questions are not aimed at accomplishing the objectives. *How, why, who, when,* and *where* questions will usually help to focus the students' thinking on the objectives.

Questions should be a challenge to the students if they are to stimulate thinking. A good oral question is similar to one on a written test; it will stimulate the students to use their knowledge to produce a proper response. Questions requiring a *yes* or *no* response or a short answer may be guessed correctly 50 percent of the time.

The final characteristic of a good question is that it is limited to one idea at a time. Rather than asking, What are the five characteristics of a good question and explain the uses of each?, it would be better to ask, What are the five characteristics of questions? After the students have answered that question, ask, How can we as teachers use those characteristics when giving instruction?

Types of Questions

Now that the purposes of questions and their characteristics have been described, let's examine the way the questioning technique may be used in the classroom, that is, the types of questions and the situations in which they can be used.

Probably the most frequently asked question is the *direct question*. Here, the teacher asks a question, pauses, and then calls on a student to answer. The direct question will keep all students alert because they have to listen to the question and wait for the teacher to call on them. If the question is directed initially to one student, the others will lose interest because they know they won't have to answer.

An *overhead question* is asked without indicating who is to reply. Several replies should be volunteered and received, and every student who wishes to contribute should be allowed to do so. An overhead question will often stimulate a dull class and might encourage shy students, but it also weakens class control. An overhead question is not the same as a *rhetorical question*. An overhead question is used to spur discussion; rhetorical questions are answered by the teacher and are used to disperse information. Quite often, rhetorical questions won't even have a correct answer.

A *reverse question* is one that is used to answer student questions by asking the question back. When the student asks, Why does this thing work this way?, the teacher can respond with a question such as, Why do you think it works this way? The intent here is not to mock the student, but to stimulate critical or analytical thinking.

If the reverse question produces discomfort or no answer, the *relay question* can be used. In this case the student's question is passed on by restating it and asking it to another student. This technique allows the teacher to remain in the background and at the same time promote class discussion.

Techniques for Questioning

Many hints about asking questions have been given as we discussed the purposes, characteristics, and types of questions. One effective technique for directing questions to students has five steps.

First, *ask* the question aloud to the entire class. After the question has been asked, *pause* for a few moments and look around the room. This allows time for all students to think of an answer. Then, *call on* one student by name. *Listen* carefully and attentively to the student's answer. If it is correct, *emphasize it* so that all students understand. If the answer is incorrect, or only partially correct, there are two choices. The first is to thank the student for trying and say something like, That's not quite what I had in mind. Can someone else help? Then pause and ask someone else. The second choice would be to ask another, more specific question to the student who incorrectly answered. Remember to praise or thank the students. We all need our pats on the back.

After the pause stage of questioning, randomly distribute questions. If students are called on in a fixed order, they will soon learn the sequence and may pay attention only when about to be called upon. The number and difficulty of questions should be distributed fairly among the students.

If there is one rule for questioning, it might be stated as follows: The ultimate purpose for asking questions is to further the students' learning. Questions that are designed to trick students or that have nothing to do with reaching the lesson objectives have no place in good instruction.

Summary

Questions have several purposes, mainly to stimulate and guide student thinking. Good classroom questions are purposeful, clear, concise, challenging, related to the objective, and limited to one idea. There are five basic types of questions, including: direct, overhead, rhetorical, reverse, and relay. An effective technique for using questions is to ask the question, pause, call on a student, listen attentively, and emphasize the correct answer.

Instructional Aids

Much has been written in this chapter about teaching techniques. Most of the material has been concerned with the teacher's personal attributes and manner in which they assist or cause students to learn. The learning process is complex, and many times words alone are not sufficient to reach the predetermined objectives established for the student. Teachers, in addition to everything else, must be knowledgeable in the development, preparation, and use of instructional aids.

For our purposes, instructional aids are defined as any device or printed material used by the teacher to assist in the attainment of lesson objectives. Instructional aids then include machines, films, chalkboards or whiteboards, flipcharts, mock-ups, charts, graphs, maps, blueprints, simulators, filmstrips and slides, audio or visual recorders, television, computers, textbooks, and printed diagrams and procedure sheets.

The reasons for using instructional aids have been discussed (realism, attention, multisensual, simplicity, clarity), and, therefore, only the most common of the instructional aids and rules for their use will be discussed here.

Chalkboard or Whiteboard

Technology has changed the blackboard to the chalkboard and now to the whiteboard. Chalkboards are usually green, but they also come in black, buff, and blue. Some are magnetic so small magnets will stay in place for materials. Some move vertically, and some slide sideways to give more working surface. Chalkboards and whiteboards are presented in this section together because the rules for their use are so similar. Unless noted otherwise, the term chalkboard includes whiteboard and vice versa. Chalkboards are particularly useful for introducing new words or phrases, indicating procedural steps, emphasizing key points, showing groups of information and relationships, and giving lesson assignments. The chalkboard may also be used to list questions, present graphs or charts, or illustrate operating principles of tools, instruments, or equipment.

There are several rules for using chalkboards. First, arrange students so that they can see the board and are not hindered by glare from the lighting. Keep material simple, and space ideas and illustrations far enough apart to avoid confusion.

Plan important chalkboard illustrations before class. When using chalkboards, write or print legibly and spell correctly. Avoid using abbreviations unless you are sure that all students know what they mean. Use colored chalk (or pens) to add emphasis to special or important points (yellow is the most visible on the green chalkboards), but don't overdo this. Most colored chalk is messy, and the use of too much color will clutter the drawing or illustration. Whiteboard pens of all colors are manufactured to a standard so they are not messy. If you have complicated drawings to show, prepare them ahead of class or use an overhead projector.

Use a clean board and avoid talking to the class while writing on the board. When using the board, speak first, then turn around and write or draw. When materials are no longer needed, erase them, or they may prove distracting later in the lesson. Form the habit of always cleaning the board before use and after you finish each section of a presentation. If you clean the board with long vertical strokes as you walk backward, you can continue to teach without missing a beat.

When writing or drawing, grasp the chalk or whiteboard pen with at least your thumb and first two fingers. Use horizontal (toward your writing hand), and vertical (top to bottom) strokes whenever possible. Circular strokes, movement away from your writing hand, or improper grip on the chalk each have a tendency to cause bone-chilling squeaks when you use the chalkboard. Most whiteboard pens dry very quickly, so recap the pen immediately after writing, or it will be difficult to start it the next time (in other words, do not use the pen as a pointer without recapping it!).

If your lesson calls for a series of illustrations and you are right-handed, it is to the students' advantage if you start at the upper right of the board and work left—the opposite of writing. This keeps your body from hiding the work. A pointer or yardstick used as a pointer is a great help in chalk and whiteboard work. Used as an extension of your arm, the pointer holds attention on the item under discussion while allowing you to maintain face-to-face communication with the class. Chalk and whiteboards are ever-ready visual aids. Their uses are limited only by the walls around your imagination.

Mock-Ups

Mock-ups can be parts of machines or systems that are removed and artificially operated for the purpose of demonstration. They might also be imitations, or representations, of parts. Mock-ups are commonly used in automobile mechanics to teach basic functions such as the electrical system. Many of the health care occupations use mock-ups of the human body or its parts.

When developing or selecting mock-ups and actual equipment, there are several factors to consider. First, keep in mind that all actions in the classroom should be an aid to student learning. Those things or objects that will help students understand more clearly should be used when and where they will be most effective. Mock-ups should be realistic, simple enough for students to understand, available at the time when they are needed, and attractive in design, color, and appearance.

Charts

The most common charts are flip charts, usually mounted on an easel for ease in turning from one to the next. Illustrative devices on paper or stiff cardboard are also called charts or diagrams. Charts or diagrams may be used for a variety of illustrative material, including schematics, pictures, tables, cartoons, and outlines of ideas or steps in a procedure.

It is difficult to stand beside a flip chart while explaining it to a class. This problem can be reduced or eliminated if an outline or general sketch of the material the class is seeing is placed on the back of the preceding sheet. This provides a built-in *cue sheet* for the teacher and allows for standing slightly to the rear of the chart. This technique also helps provide all students with an unobstructed view of the chart.

Filmstrips and Slides

There are only a few occupations for which filmstrips and slides are not available commercially. Both are much more economical and easier to use than motion pictures, and since the frames are projected one at a time, they allow for as much or as little discussion as necessary. Most universities with teacher education programs have courses in how to prepare filmstrip and slide presentations.

Filmstrips and slides should be appropriate, realistic, attractive, and focused on the objective. A poor filmstrip is worse than none at all. Some techniques for getting the most benefit from filmstrips and slides are included in this chapter in the section on films.

Transparencies

One of the revolutionary items invented and then adapted for use in teaching was the overhead projector. The uses for this compact, inexpensive machine are limited only by one's imagination. For example, with the overhead projector, transparencies for projection can be prepared in advance, only the complex parts of complex transparencies needed can be used, they can be written on as a lesson progresses, they can be erased and reused, they can be filed with the lesson plan, they are used in lighted classrooms, and the teacher can face the class while writing on the transparency. There is generally no need for assistants when using overhead transparencies, but if you are teaching an extremely large group and an assistant is needed, it is necessary to have some system of signals so the assistant will know when to change the transparency.

Transparent acetate slides can be purchased for use as transparencies, but common, plastic document protectors that have been split to produce two sheets are often as good. Grease pencils, drafting ink, and felt markers will all produce images. Grease pencil of any color will always project black, but felt markers of different colors will project the color.

The overhead projector is probably the most versatile of the projection media. The teacher controls the pace, selection, emphasis, and review. The projector will project transparent or opaque objects, animated devices and fluids, as well as transparencies. Details can be pointed to on the transparencies, and the teacher can write or draw on them. Transparencies eliminate repetitive chalkboard work, thereby making available more classroom time for instruction and review. Another valuable asset of the overhead projector is that the on-off switch can be used to control and direct the attention of the class. Be sure, though, to turn the projector off when you are through with each transparency to eliminate distraction.

Films and Videos

Educational films and videos differ from Hollywood films in that they have been carefully produced for a specific instructional purpose. To ensure that students receive the utmost benefit from films, videos, and other projection materials, including slides and transparencies, several techniques are helpful.

First, always preview the material. By being familiar with the content, the teacher will be able to tie it in to the previous lessons and tell the students what they are expected to learn from it.

All equipment should be thoroughly checked prior to class time. Load the projector or video player so that a flip of the switch will have the materials on the screen.

Some commercial materials may have extraneous information in them that will have to be removed by editing or bypassing. This is next to impossible in films. Some classes may require more detailed information than available in the visual aid, so the teacher will have to be prepared to supplement it with other material or by explanation.

Visual material is just like any other part of a lesson—it has to be introduced. Tell students a little about the content and what they are expected to learn. If they know what to look for, they will be more likely to recognize it when they see it.

Explain why the material is being shown. There should be some good reason why class time is being used to present it. Instructional aids are used to help the students reach the objectives of the lesson.

When a film or video is long, it is a good practice to stop it at a convenient place and discuss the points covered. When the presentation is over, it is not enough to stop there. Follow up the presentation with written or oral questions and provide additional description and explanation as needed.

Computers

The use of computers in occupational instruction could be likened to the turtle in the classic turtle and hare story. Like the turtle, the use of computers has steadily gained ground on some of the other uses of technology in the classroom. The most obvious use of computers in occupational education is in the teaching of computer-related technical skills, but new software is appearing on a regular basis that can be used in teaching almost all other occupational skills, including nontechnical skills such as interpersonal behavior. Personal computers also have myriad other uses for teachers and can make their jobs easier. The most popular uses in the classroom today include word processing, graphics production, program evaluation, budget control, test scoring, and record keeping. Computers can also be used to process data from all of those follow-up surveys occupational teachers have to do and to keep track of student projects. Teacher licensing laws in many states now include computer literacy as one of the competencies new teachers are required to demonstrate.

Computer hardware and software for educational use seems to be everywhere.

Computerized instructional programs are generally referred to as computer-assisted instruction, or CAI. Most early CAI programs were merely electronic page-turners and were structured in very small bites in the manner of programmed instruction. The advent of CD-ROM, more powerful multimedia computers, and better programming has led to the development of stunning, interactive instructional materials, including some that simulate three-dimensional reality. Multimedia and computer-assisted instructional material is still expensive when compared to other forms of learning materials, but more and more universities and professional associations are creating and distributing multimedia material specifically designed by and for educators at lower costs. Find these materials and use them as you would any other instructional aid.

Audio and Visual Recorders

Audio and visual recorders are used to record special lectures and speeches, presentations of other teachers, explanation and discussions by students, and the sounds and noises of engines, instruments, and other operating equipment. Entire new worlds are opening up with increased use of instructional television, including "packaging" of entire lessons or courses, and close-up views of complicated operations or procedures conducted in confined spaces. The rules for using audio and visual recorders and recordings are the same as for other projected instructional aids.

Printed Instructional Aids

Printed aids include procedure sheets, reproductions of charts, reference tables, diagrams, maps, and pictures. Many of these aids are available commercially, but most are teacher-made. Printed instructional aids should have a definite purpose, be easy to follow, legible, and use language properly. Printed or graphic materials should be clearly labeled; and if they are taken from another source such as a book or magazine, the source should be credited.

Summary

Instructional aids offer the opportunity to dramatize and clarify classroom presentations. The aids themselves are neutral; it is what the teacher does with them that counts. Technical assistance is available in the selection and development of instructional aids in most schools, school districts, and universities with teacher education programs. All aids should have a definite, well-thought-out purpose and should relate to and clarify course or lesson objectives.

For Further Reading

Brown, J.W., Lewis, R.B., and Harcleroad, F.F. (1983). *AV Instruction: Technology, Media, and Methods.* New York: McGraw-Hill.

Brown, J.W., and Lewis, R.B. (1983). *AV Instructional Technology Manual for Independent Study.* New York: McGraw-Hill.

Calderon, M. (1989). "Cooperative Learning for LEP Students." Center for Research on the Education of Disadvantaged Students, UCSB/Johns Hopkins.

Cell, E. (1984). *Learning to Learn from Experience.* Albany, NY: State University of New York Press.

Dickinson, G. (1973). *Teaching Adults: A Handbook for Instructors.* Toronto: New Press.

Goodlad, J.I., Soder, R., and Sirotnik, K.A. (1990). *The Moral Dimensions of Teaching.* San Francisco: Jossey-Bass.

Joyce, B., and Weil, M. (1986). *Models of Teaching.* Third Edition. Englewood Cliffs, NJ: Prentice-Hall.

Kasworm, C.E. (1983). "An Examination of Self-Directed Contract Learning as an Instructional Strategy." *Innovative Higher Education* 8(1):45–54.

Kilgore, K., Ross, D., and Zbikowski, J. (1990). "Understanding the Teaching Perspectives of First-Year Teachers." *Journal of Teacher Education* 41:28(11).

Knowles, M. (1970). *Modern Practice of Adult Education.* New York: Association Press.

Knowles, M. (1975). *Self-Directed Learning: A Guide for Learners and Teachers.* New York: Association Press.

Knox, A.B. (1986). *Helping Adults Learn: A Guide to Planning, Implementing, and Conducting Programs.* San Francisco: Jossey-Bass.

Koschmann, T.D., Myers, A.C., Feltovich, P.J., and Barrows, H.S. (1994). "Technology to Assist in Realizing Effective Learning and Instruction: A Principled Approach to the Use of Computers in Collaborative Learning." *Journal of the Learning Sciences* 3:227–264.

Leighbody, G.B., and Kidd, D.M. (1968). *Methods of Teaching Shop and Related Subjects.* Albany, NY: Delmar.

Miller, H., and Vinocur, S. (1973). "How To Ask Classroom Questions." *School and Community* 59(6):10.

Miller, W.R., and Rose, H. (1975). *Instructors and Their Jobs.* Chicago: American Technical Society.

Nystrom, D.C., Bayne, G.K., and McClellan, L.D. (1977). *Instructional Methods in Occupational Education.* Indianapolis: Bobbs-Merrill Publishing.

Robenstein, J. (1986). *Microcomputers in Vocational Education.* Englewood Cliffs, NJ: Prentice-Hall.

Schmidt, B.J. (1984, Winter). "Procedures for Evaluating Microcomputer Software Used in Vocational Education." *Journal of Vocational Education Research* 9(1):10–23.

Smith, R.M. (1982). *Learning How To Learn: Applied Theory for Adults.* New York: Cambridge Book Company.

Skinner, B.F. (1968). *The Technology of Teaching.* New York: Appleton-Century-Crofts.

Vaughn, J. (1986, September). "Finding the Right Software." *Vocational Education Journal* 61(6):37–38.

Wilen, William W. (Ed.) (1987). *Questions, Questioning Techniques, and Effective Teaching.* Washington, DC: National Education Association.

Discussion Questions

Communication

1. Why is a common core of experience a necessity for effective communication in the classroom?

   _____

   _____

   _____

2. How can gestures and movements be consistent with facial expressions and posture in portraying the feeling or attitude of the teacher?

   _____

   _____

   _____

3. How can gestures and movement enhance oral communication?

   _____

   _____

   _____

4. Why is it important to establish direct eye contact with students when making classroom presentations?

   _____

   _____

   _____

Instructional Techniques

5. When is it most advisable to use the lecture method of instruction? Why?

   _____

   _____

   _____

6. Why should visual aids be used with the lecture method of teaching?

   _____

   _____

   _____

7. When presenting a lesson using the lecture method, an overview is given in the introduction and motivation. Why should key points be emphasized in the body of the lesson?

   _____

   _____

   _____

8. How does a guided discussion differ from a lecture?

_____

_____

_____

9. In what teaching situations is discussion an appropriate teaching method?

_____

_____

_____

10. Why is a permissive atmosphere important for a successful discussion? How might a teacher create a permissive atmosphere?

_____

_____

_____

11. Why is the demonstration method considered teacher-centered?

_____

_____

_____

12. In what ways does the teacher's demonstration affect student performance?

_____

_____

_____

13. Are the cognitive skills such as facts, figures, and their associations taught when using the demonstration method? How?

_____

_____

_____

14. When using the student performance method, why is it necessary to evaluate student procedures as well as the end product?

_____

_____

_____

15. How can student performance problems or projects be made realistic? Give examples from your occupational area.

_____

_____

_____

16. Programmed instruction is best used with what type of information? Why?

_____

_____

_____

Use of Questions

17. Why are questions used in instruction?

_____

_____

_____

18. Why are questions that can be answered with a _yes_ or _no_ of little value in a discussion?

_____

_____

_____

19. Why should a question be asked before any student is called upon?

_____

_____

_____

20. How can questioning be used as an aid in evaluating student comprehension?

_____

_____

_____

21. What principle of learning is supported through the use of questions?

_____

_____

_____

Instructional Aids

22. Assume that a friend who knows nothing about teaching asks you what an instructional aid is. What will you tell them?

_____

_____

_____

23. If you had a choice between two different instructional aids and one was much more realistic than the other but did not directly relate to the lesson objectives, which one would you select? Why?

_____

_____

_____

24. Why it is important to erase or remove from view material that is not related to the lesson at hand?

_____

_____

_____

Exercises

1. Define _abstraction_ and give an example from the occupation.

_____

_____

_____

2. Describe three verbal mannerisms common to everyday speech that will interfere with clarity of presentation.

   a. _____

   b. _____

   c. _____

3. List the three elements of the process of communication.

   a. _____

   b. _____

   c. _____

4. List the four qualities of voice control that affect the quality of communication.

    a. _____

    b. _____

    c. _____

    d. _____

Instructional Techniques

5. List the four major limitations of the lecture method of instruction, and then list a possible method of minimizing each limitation.

    a. _____ minimized by _____

    b. _____ minimized by _____

    c. _____ minimized by _____

    d. _____ minimized by _____

6. List the four major distinct parts of a discussion lesson and describe the purpose of each.

    a._____ whose purpose is_____

    b._____ whose purpose is_____

    c._____ whose purpose is_____

    d._____ whose purpose is_____

7. Name five situations from teaching your occupation in which the demonstration method would be appropriate.

    a. _____

    b. _____

    c. _____

    d. _____

    e. _____

8. Compare the advantages and disadvantages of the student performance method of instruction in teaching your occupation.

    _____

    _____

    _____

9. List the seven most common purposes for using questions in instruction and relate them to a principle of learning or a learning theory.

    a. _____

    _____

b. _____

_____

c. _____

_____

d. _____

_____

e. _____

_____

f. _____

_____

g. _____

_____

10. List the four characteristics of a good question.

a. _____

b. _____

c. _____

d. _____

11. List the five steps used in asking a question in class.

a. _____

b. _____

c. _____

d. _____

e. _____

12. Following is a list of various instructional techniques, situations, or methods of teaching. Based on the course you teach, select topics that would best be taught using the methods listed. Consider the things you have learned about learning theory, styles of learning, and styles of teaching.

a. The improved lecture, including visual aids and methods to check on learning.

_____

b. Teacher demonstrations.

_____

c. Teacher-guided discussion.

_____

d. Skeleton outline of the lesson with space for students to fill in notes (also called _controlled notes_).

_____

e. Students-to-teacher feedback by use of closely spaced questions answered by all students (commonly called _drill_).

_____

f. Supervised study within the classroom when students, individually or in small groups, are assisted by the teacher.

_____

g. Student panels.

_____

h. Role-portraying (role-playing).

_____

i. Motion picture, video, or filmstrip with the whole class.

_____

j. Filmstrip or slides used on a self-study assignment.

_____

k. Television program, either during class time or outside of class, and report to class.

_____

l. Resource speakers.

_____

m. Computer-assisted instruction.

_____

n. Research and report.

_____

o. Student experiments.

_____

p. Student projects.

_____

13. Prepare a list of community resource speakers who can make a worthy contribution or provide a valid learning experience for your students. Always secure approval in advance from the resource persons before you list them in your resource guide. A suggested format with the necessary information may be found in the appendix.

14. Using a local public (or school or university) library, business promotional materials, your school's audiovisual center, and any other source, compile a list of audiovisual resources that will be valuable in teaching your occupation to others. A suggested Audiovisual Resources form for compiling the list may be found in the appendix. Devise a scale and rate each item for content, clarity, and usefulness.

15. Using the Lesson Observation Rating Form, which is found in the appendix, observe two classes taught by another teacher, preferably at a school other than your own. (a) Try to observe classes that have students like yours (i.e., adults, high school, industrial training). (b) Observe one class that is commonly considered academic, such as English or mathematics, and one class that is considered occupational education. (c) Secure the permission of the school or program administrators prior to making the observation. They may even be able to suggest good teachers to observe. Tell the administrators and teachers why you are making the observation.

7 How Do You Know That You Did What You Set Out to Do?

Some Techniques of Evaluation

You will recall from previous chapters that evaluation is an integral part of the learning process—a lesson or a unit of instruction is not complete until the extent of the students' learning has been determined. If our objectives have been properly specified, whenever learning takes place, the result should be a definable, observable, and measurable change in behavior. The evaluation process is concerned with defining, observing, measuring, and judging this behavior. During the discussion in Chapter 6 of the various instructional techniques, it was recommended that the teacher observe the students' reactions during the presentation and to periodically ask them questions to check their understanding. These activities are a form of evaluation, and they indicate that evaluation occurs at many points in teaching and learning, not just at the end.

Many people view evaluation as some exotic, complicated process, but the reality is that we all engage in evaluation activities everyday. We judge the merits of the weather, the fit of our clothes, and how our car's engine performs. These informal, and often unconscious, efforts at evaluation are all attempts to determine the worth of something. This everyday evaluation process is usually informal and unconscious. Teachers make these informal evaluations in the school situation when, for example, they listen to a piece of equipment and decide that it is running poorly, or when they walk into a classroom for the first time and sense intuitively the tenor of the group.

The teacher's evaluation of student learning and performance cannot be an informal process. Administrative demands and the students' right to know the criteria upon which their grades are based require that evaluation in the classroom be a formal, objective process of measurement. Formal evaluation in the classroom is usually done by using tests, by students evaluating their own performance against some standard or checklist, by peers, and, increasingly more so, by persons external to the classroom who evaluate portfolios of the students' work. Other methods of evaluating the quality of the learning achieved by students include assessment of their written and manipulative work, systematic teacher observation, diagnostic assessments conducted by other trained personnel, and even use of standardized tests.

Tests and other assessments to determine student achievement are but two of the ways evaluation is used in education. Teachers evaluate themselves and each other in order to determine their effectiveness, and entire programs are evaluated in terms of their cost, the rate of placement of students, and their overall effectiveness.

This chapter deals with the first two kinds of evaluation: tests for determining student achievement and instructional evaluation. A complete discussion of test construction and student assessment is beyond the scope of this text, so the reader is advised to take courses and consult the references found at the end of the chapter. The reasons for conducting different types of evaluation and techniques for evaluating performance are discussed in the following sections.

Evaluation of Student Achievement

The evaluation process usually includes the use of written tests that are prepared by the teacher specifically to determine the students' cognitive gain. Performance tests are prepared to determine exactly how well the students can perform the physical or manipulative activities detailed in the course objectives. Tests vary in length and importance, and they may be administered in formal or informal manners.

Teachers are responsible for developing individual test items; preparing, administering, and scoring the examinations; and evaluating the results. Each of these responsibilities is examined in the subsequent paragraphs, but first a look at the purposes of testing is appropriate.

Purposes of Testing

The basic purpose of testing in occupational education is to determine how well the students have learned the subject matter of the course. Several important secondary purposes include providing an objective basis for grades, determining what areas of the subject may need to be retaught, determining whether students are ready to advance to the next unit of instruction, and assisting in reinforcing learning and motivating students.

Grades.   Teachers usually have to assign course marks, or grades, to students at specific times. Test grades help the teacher make these determinations, but they should not be the sole basis for grades. Other factors to consider in grading are the results of graded classroom activities, prepared assignments, and rate and degree of improvement. The teacher's personal evaluation of the student as a future employee, although subjective, is a very important factor.

Reteaching.   Teacher analysis of test results may reveal that the students are weak in specific areas of the subject matter. Because schedules of instruction usually have little "slack" time, special assignments may have to be made to help students catch up. If the amount of material is small, the entire class might be retaught the relevant material, or out-of-class instruction might be arranged for individuals or small groups.

Advancement.   If the test results indicate that one or more students are not ready to advance to the next unit of instruction, provision should be made for them to repeat whatever instruction is necessary. This procedure is definitely recommended in any case where the unlearned subject matter is requisite for the understanding of material taught in the next or later unit of instruction.

Reinforcement.   One of the principles of learning states that those things often repeated are best remembered. Tests help the teacher to require students to remember and apply knowledge, thereby reinforcing their learning. Tests also help motivate students by providing them with an incentive for putting forth their best efforts.

Qualities of Good Tests

A good test should be valid, reliable, objective, and practical. Of these criteria, assuming that a test is based on course objectives, validity is the most important.

Test Validity.   The term validity is used to indicate the degree to which a test or test item (question) measures what it is supposed to measure. For an entire test to be valid, every item must be related to the stated objective *and* must measure the degree of behavior change sought. Other factors that might affect the validity of test results are the manner in which the test is administered, the physical and emotional condition of the students, and the quality of the instruction. Some tests with long, detailed instructions or written questions are often less valid because they measure the students' ability to read rather than perform. Other tests are less valid because they were written by one teacher for one group of students and were administered by another teacher to another group of students.

Reliability.   This term is used to express the degree to which a test gives consistent results each time it is given, provided the classes to which the test is given are of the same ability level and that the test is given each time under like, or similar conditions. Reliability is difficult to guarantee, especially the first time the test is given, but several practices help. First, the test should be long enough to provide thorough coverage of the subject matter. Short tests increase the chance that only familiar items were covered. Second, elements that will increase the chance of guessing correctly should be eliminated. (We will discuss this further under types of test items.) To help guarantee reliability, when giving performance tests, make certain that all equipment used in the test is in approximately the same condition.

Objectivity.   The term objectivity refers to the degree to which a test can be scored without bias or the personal opinion of the scorer affecting the grades. In other words, a person who has little or no knowledge of the subject matter should be able to score the tests using a ready-made key.

Practicability.   This term is used to describe the extent to which a test is usable. This includes the test's readability, its ease of administration and scoring, and the time, material, money, and personnel required. Tests that are poorly duplicated or make excessive demands on time and personnel are not practical.

Objective Tests

Learning occurs in three domains: the cognitive, the affective, and the psychomotor. To determine learning in the cognitive domain, some form of written or oral test is usually given. Some learning in the affective domain may be determined using written or oral tests, but often it is necessary to observe the students' behavior over a period of time. Learning in the psychomotor domain *must* be determined through the use of a performance (doing) examination.

Each of the common types of test items are described. A very brief description of the item, its advantages and disadvantages, and some tips for constructing them are presented. The reader is advised to consult other references and to take courses in test construction to gain a thorough knowledge of how to write tests. The final paragraphs of this section contain some pointers on constructing complete tests and some rules for their administration and scoring. A sample examination may be found in the appendix. Some of the items on the sample examination cover material found in this book; other items are from various occupational subjects.

True-False

True-false tests are one of five basic kinds of written tests used to determine student achievement in the cognitive domain. They consist of a series of statements. The students are asked to indicate whether the statements are true or false. True-false tests are easy to design, easy to score, and can be used to cover a wide range of material quickly. True-false tests are apt to be low in reliability, and they often measure students' reading ability rather than their knowledge of the subject matter. In addition, students have a 50-50 chance of guessing the correct answer on each item. Specific determiners, or words such as *never* and *always* when used in the statements increase the guess factor because very few things are *always*. On the other hand, attempts to soften the wording also serve as hints to the correct answer.

To decrease the chance that students will guess on true-false items and to check the depth of their understanding, have students underline the word or phrase that will make it true. This will make the tests more difficult to score, but it pays off in increased value of the test. Using this method, students are given more opportunity to express what they really know.

Multiple-Choice

Multiple-choice test items consist of a statement or a question followed by a list of choices, only one of which is correct. They can be used to test knowledge of factual information or understanding of the subject matter. Multiple-choice items reduce the chance of guessing the correct answer, and they are easy to score. A disadvantage of some multiple-choice items is that students are only required to recognize the correct answer, not recall it. You will remember that recognition is a lower level of learning than recall. Like true-false items, multiple-choice tests may measure students' reading ability rather than knowledge.

There are several rules to follow when constructing multiple-choice items. First, the introductory statement should express a problem or a complete question. Sufficient information should be included in the stem, or lead, to clearly indicate what the problem is before the student reaches the choices.

Second, at least four, but not more than six, choices from which to select an answer should be given. Choices should be in grammatical agreement with the stem of the item, and all choices should relate to the same area of the subject matter.

All choices offered should be plausible. If one or more choices are impossible or ridiculous, the student can immediately eliminate them from consideration, and the item becomes easier to answer. If you cannot think of enough plausible choices, use the question for a true-false or completion item.

When choices consist of numbers, they should be arranged in numerical order, either ascending or descending. The correct choices should not habitually be longer than the other choices. An occasional long phrase is permissible, but if one occurs often, the students soon realize that the reason one choice is longer is because it has been expanded to ensure that it will be true.

It is a good practice to write multiple-choice test items on an index card as you think of them. Key the card to lesson or course objectives by using a number or letter code in one corner of the card, then file the card until you are ready to compile the test. This practice also works well with other types of questions.

Completion

A completion test item consists of a statement with one or more key words missing and blanks left in their place. Students are required to fill in the blanks. If the question is one that can be answered very briefly, it may be put in the form of a completed question followed by a blank space.

With this type of question, there is little chance for students to guess the correct answer, and completion items test students' ability to recall rather than to recognize. They are good to use when students must be able to remember facts, words, or symbols. It is, however, difficult to create statements that call for only one correct answer.

When constructing completion items, try to omit only one key word or phrase and avoid having the blank come near the beginning of the statement. For phrases, use a long blank rather than several short blanks, but be sure that the directions indicate that a phrase is expected for long blanks. For one word answers, the blanks in all items should be of the same length. Items taken directly from class or text material will encourage needless memorizing. Construct statements that require thought.

Identification

An identification item is one in which students are required to recognize such things as tools, materials, and parts of equipment and then identify that item in writing. Pictures or drawings are necessary in written identification tests, so reproduction is sometimes a problem. Identification test items measure recognition and recall. Sometimes teachers require students to briefly state the purpose or use of each identified item in addition to naming it. This practice determines some depth of understanding, but students who have difficulty expressing themselves sometimes falter on these items.

Matching

Matching tests consist of two lists of related words, symbols, or phrases. The students are required to match the items in accordance with the instructions. A large number of responses can be obtained in one matching test item, but they are difficult to write properly. Matching items are very objective and discriminating, but they are not the best method for measuring complete understanding of information and judgment.

When using matching items it is important that the instructions are clear and concise, telling the students what to match with what. The items in the left list should be limited to a single subject matter category, and the choices in the right list should be limited to a single category. The choices should be arranged in a systematic order (such as alphabetically) in order to help the student who knows the correct answer to quickly locate it.

The number of items to be matched should be no less than five and no more than twelve. If there are less than five, it would be best to use completion items or a series of multiple-choice items. More than twelve items tends to cause confusion.

There should always be more choices than there are items to be matched. An exception can be made when one or more choices may be used more than once.

Short Answer Essay

Essay questions are not particularly suitable to occupational education, largely because they place a premium on students' abilities to express themselves in writing, rather than in their ability to practically apply the knowledge or skills that have been taught. If students will be required to write reports or descriptions on the job, the essay examination is one way of determining their ability to do so. The main disadvantage of an essay, or short answer essay examination, is that it is hard to grade objectively. It is also time-consuming to correct, and it may encourage bluffing. These disadvantages can be overcome by asking for specific information that can be written in a short paragraph. The basis of the answer, particularly in questions that ask the students to discuss something, should be given.

Make sure that the question is clear and that the students know exactly what is expected. Require the students to explain *why* in their answers and to describe and give reasons for the answers. When used appropriately, the essay item provides a means of measuring students' abilities to organize subject matter, to discuss it comprehensively, and to draw conclusions.

Performance Tests

In occupational education, the performance test is the ultimate answer to the question, How do you know that you did what you set out to do? The aim of all occupational education is to provide people with the skills, knowledge, and attitudes necessary for success on the job. We cannot know whether they possess the skills, knowledge, and attitudes until we see them demonstrated. Performance tests are designed to measure the student's skill in performing a particular job in its entirety or a procedure that is part of a more complicated job. There will always be a body of knowledge that is related to the performance being tested, but the knowledge will usually be measured using written tests. Some attitudinal items may be measured, or observed, during a performance test. Attitudes necessary for success on the job can be recorded on the checklist or rating sheet for performance tests that is discussed below.

Performance tests will vary in form and content since every skill presents a different problem of measurement. They will also vary according to the accuracy of measurement desired. For example, some tests are designed to indicate whether or not a skill has been developed to an acceptable level, while other tests must quantitatively measure the degree of skill acquired. An example of the former test is a strength requirement used in some civil service occupations—can a person carry a heavy object for X number of feet? The performance test will show that they either can or cannot. An example of the latter test (a quantitative measurement) is a typing test that determines not only that a person can type, but also how many words per minute with how many errors. Teacher-administered performance tests are usually conducted using a checklist or an examination of a finished product. When using a checklist or rating sheet, the student performs the job while the teacher observes the performance and records the results on a checklist that has all the steps and standards of performance on it. The finished product performance examination is one in which the student produces or repairs something that the teacher evaluates upon completion.

To prepare a performance test, it is necessary to select or design a job that is essential to course objectives and can be accomplished with available time, resources, and equipment. Then describe exactly what is to be tested, such as accuracy, skill, speed, or other traits of the job.

The next step is to list the operations that are necessary to perform the work covered by the test. You might wish to refer to your task analysis for this (see Chapter 5). The checklist should also include standards of measurement, time allowed, and other key points critical to safe and accurate performance.

A list of tools, materials, drawings, and equipment that will be needed to perform the test should be made. This will serve two purposes: first, it will serve as your check in setting up the test, and second, it will save students from having to gather everything. If a grade is to be assigned to the test, a scoring system will have to be devised. This should be shared with and explained to the students prior to taking the test.

When giving the test, make sure that all students have all the required tools and materials and that they understand exactly what they are to do and how they will be rated. Working conditions should be identical for all test-takers. When checking work, use the same tools or measuring instruments that the students used to perform the work. Other than to clarify instructions, do not offer any assistance or intervene during the test unless a student is in danger of hurting himself or others.

Test Construction

All items in all tests should be valid, reliable, objective, and practical. They *must* relate to and measure behavior that is specified in the objectives. The types of items used in any one test should be chosen with an understanding of student ability, the nature of the subject matter, the course objectives, and the time available. Some general rules for test construction follow.

Objectives.   Select specific objectives to be measured. If they are in the cognitive domain, a written examination will be necessary. Some cognitive ability or knowledge can be surmised from actions on a performance test, but construction of the checklist to determine this is difficult and may make observation of more than one student at a time impossible. A good rule of thumb to follow is: If it's cognitive, use a written test.

Outline.   Develop an outline of the test that you are going to construct. Do this in the same fashion that you would a lesson plan in order to make sure that all objectives are tested.

Construct Items.   Write the actual test items, putting each item on an individual index card. Indicate the correct answer on the card. It is also a good idea to note somewhere on the card the objective that the item is written for. For any given test, prepare 25 to 50 percent more items than will be needed. This will allow you to easily throw away ambiguous or poorly worded items.

Assemble the Test.   The first item needed on any test is a set of general instructions. In these instructions tell the students the purpose of the test and the type of questions they will encounter. If you do not want them to write on the test itself, tell them so here. Inform them that specific instructions will be provided for each type of question.

Next, group all items by type. Put all true-false items in one stack, all multiple-choice in another, and so on. This is easy if you have put each item on an index card. Now prepare a set of instructions for each type of question. Tell the students in these instructions what the items consist of and how they are to indicate the answer.

Read through all items of each type and weed out those that supply answers to other questions. Also, omit items that are dependent on answers to other questions because with such questions a slight mistake is doubled. The student may know the correct procedure or process, but a wrong answer to the first part also gets them a wrong answer to the second part.

Answers to questions should form a random pattern. Many of us have favorite letters that we unconsciously use as the correct answer when making up test items. Examine your items to detect this tendency and rearrange as necessary.

When placing the test on paper, no question or answer group should extend from one page to the next. Multiple-choice answer possibilities should be

DRABBLE By Kevin Fagan

arranged vertically rather than run all together. This will require a bit more paper to reproduce the test, but it will be much easier to read and to take. Remember, the purpose of testing is to determine students' achievement, not their ability to wade through a maze of words.

Use as many items as necessary to cover the subject or the objectives. It is not a sin to have odd numbers of items on a test. Items at all levels of difficulty should be used but start the test with an easy item. This will get everyone off to a good, successful start.

Ensure that each item is realistic and practical by reviewing the assembled test one more time. If an item is not good, eliminate it before reproducing the test.

Finally, prepare an answer sheet omitting the questions. This allows you to correct the test without turning hundreds of pages and trying to match items with your key. Many teachers who ignore this last rule find out two-thirds of the way through correcting an examination that on the third paper they "corrected" their key from a student's paper! Needless to say, they have to start over.

Most teachers will prepare tests for specific lessons or units of instruction. If the course is taught over and over and the test is word-processed, it is an easy matter to bring up the test the next time it is needed and adjust it according to what was covered in the unit by adding or subtracting items. Computers and word processing have helped make test construction a pleasant process. If you are a more sophisticated computer user and have sufficient computers in your classroom, there are many good programs that will help you administer the test without paper.

Administering the Test

The validity and reliability of any test are affected to some extent by the conditions under which it is given. The test area should be well lighted, ventilated, and quiet. All materials necessary for taking the test should be provided, and all materials should be the same or of equivalent quality. All students should have the opportunity of taking the same test under the best possible conditions.

The following rules for test administration are general and are recommended specifically for written tests, although they will often apply to performance tests.

Attitude. The teacher should maintain a cheerful, relaxed demeanor. Encourage the students to view the test as an opportunity rather than as a trial by fire. If this attitude prevails, students will usually do better and the results will be more valid.

Distractions. All teaching aids, chalkboard notes, and other distractions should be covered or removed. Students should be instructed to put notes and books away, unless the test is an open-book examination wherein part of the examination will test the students' ability to use reference materials.

Cheating. Take precautions to prevent cheating. Position students so that it is difficult to whisper or to see another student's paper. Do not allow materials other than those necessary to take the test to be on top of the desks or work stations. Distribute all test materials according to a seating plan. Number tests or test booklets and hand one to each student individually if possible. Make sure that each student returns the test or booklet that they were issued.

Instructions. Provide complete and clear oral instructions for taking the test. It is a good idea to read aloud any written instructions in order to ensure that all students receive the correct instructions. Often, when students are in a hurry while taking the test, they will only give superficial attention to the written instructions.

Supervision. The teacher should maintain quiet supervision of all students taking the test. Position yourself so that you can see all students and take action or move around only as the need arises. Patrolling the room gives the impression that the teacher is suspicious or distrustful and distracts the students from the task at hand.

Scoring the Test

Many schools have equipment and supplies for machine scoring tests. For the most part though, teachers have to score (or correct) tests by hand. This is why you were encouraged in previous paragraphs to develop and use separate answer sheets for each test.

A scoring stencil can be easily made for correcting multiple-choice, true-false, and matching items. Often, an answer sheet that has holes punched to indicate the correct answer will suffice. When the stencil is placed over the answer sheets, incorrectly marked answers do not show, but the unmarked correct answer shows through the hole. A simple count (after scoring) of the unmarked choices that occur at the holes is the number of answers missed by the student.

Completion, or short answer, items are usually scored by using a strip of paper that has the correct answers on it. This strip is spaced according to the blank lines on the answer sheet and is laid alongside those lines for a quick comparison of the student's answers with the correct answers.

Before scoring any tests, it is a good practice to scan all answer sheets to see if more than one answer has been marked per item. Count all items incorrect that have more than one answer marked. Use colored pencil or felt markers for correcting examinations. After using the stencil or strip sheet for correcting, total all items with two or more answers, those with incorrect answers, and those left unanswered. Subtract this total from the total number of test items. The remainder is the student's score, which should be written at the top of the answer sheet. Sometimes teachers will count multiple-choice items as double that of true-false or matching. In this case, scores have to be tallied for individual sections of the test and then totaled.

A number of excellent programs are available commercially that will help you store test items and computer-generate new tests quickly and easily. Most of these programs allow the user to pick and choose among the different test items and will automatically rotate the possible answers to different positions, so the item is different each time it is printed.

Grading

Most schools use letter grades that are based on some percentage of 100. For example, 89.5 to 100 is often considered to be an "A," 79.5 to 89.5 a "B," and so on down. It is a simple matter to define what that scale is and to convert raw test scores to a percentage and assign grades accordingly. It is very important for both teacher and student alike to remember that the assessment process and grades are *part of learning*, not the end of it. If all parties approach testing and assessment with that attitude, it is a much more pleasant experience for everyone.

Summary

A number of test items that are used to determine the extent of students' knowledge were described in this section. The most common written questions used are true-false, multiple-choice, completion, identification, and matching. Short answer essay questions may be used where appropriate to determine students' skill in organizing subject matter, discussing it, and drawing conclusions. The key test in occupational education is the performance test, wherein students are required to actually perform to accepted standards a job that they will have to do upon program completion. A sample examination that contains illustrative examples of the several types of questions may be found in the appendix.

Evaluation of Instruction

One goal of all evaluation is the improvement of instruction. The ultimate purpose of the evaluation of *instruction* is the improvement of our effectiveness as teachers. Through self-evaluation, evaluation by the students, and evaluation by our peers, we become more competent teachers and more aware of and accountable for our actions. The previous section was concerned with evaluation of student performance. This section is concerned with evaluation of teacher performance.

Most new teachers of occupational subjects will find that the first year of teaching is not unlike being blindfolded and dropped in the middle of a foreign country at midnight without a map or command of the language. We are no longer "on the job"; we are dealing with a new set of people, our colleagues all speak Educationese, and we can't reach the light switch for all the books and papers that are in the way!

When evaluating instruction, whether it is through self-evaluation, student evaluation, or peer evaluation, there are three major areas that should be examined. First, the effects of the instruction on the students should be determined. Second, the teacher's plan of teaching should be evaluated, and third, the actual performance of the teacher is evaluated. All three areas of concern in evaluation of instruction are evaluated by the students, by the teachers themselves, and by their peers.

The *effect of the instruction* on students includes the interest students display, their response in class, their success in practical activities, and test results. In the long run, we can determine teacher effect on students by examining students' success in the workplace. This, of course, requires the use of follow-up studies after graduation.

The *evaluation of teaching plans* also includes evaluating lesson plans, procedure sheets, instructional aids, texts and references, and other tangible items used in the teaching process. The lesson and course objectives that are generated as a result of job and task analysis should also be evaluated to determine whether they conform to standard practice.

An *evaluation of teacher performance* is concerned with the delivery of instruction and its subsequent follow-through. Such characteristics as clear communication, eye contact, student involvement, technical accuracy, and use of the language are examined for their effect.

Student evaluation of instruction has been a hotly debated subject for many years. Arguments presented from both sides are valid: some of it is good, some of it is not so good. The fact remains, however, that if students are irritated with something a teacher does, or clearly do not understand, then the teaching is not being effective. In most cases, students are not competent to judge the quality of the technical material being presented to them, but they are competent to judge (or at least to comment on) the effectiveness of the manner in which it was presented. This is not a place for a complete discussion of student evaluation of instruction, but generally, students are able to comment on such things as the use of productive teaching techniques, the teacher's interpersonal relations skills, the organization of the presentations, and the classroom environment.

A sample form for student evaluation of instruction may be found in the appendix, and references for others are at the end of the chapter. Choose an instrument, or adapt one for your use, and periodically administer them in your classes. Keep the evaluations anonymous, so students will feel free to respond openly. Tabulate the results and take them to heart. Then make a concerted effort to improve the areas that the students feel you need improvement in.

Self-evaluation is something we all do at nearly all times. It is a necessary adjunct to self-direction and personal discipline, both of which are characteristics that contribute to success on the job. Good teachers (who are also good welders or nurses or mechanics or . . .) always try to find ways to improve their effectiveness. One way to do this is to review every lesson after it has been taught to determine what was done well and what could have been improved. The Lesson Observation Rating Form that may be found in the appendix is one way of rating yourself, although it was designed to be used by others, particularly by peers. Another form of self-evaluation is to personally appraise whether you possess or demonstrate the traits that good teachers are *supposed* to have. Techniques and forms for doing just that may be found in several of the references listed at the end of the chapter. Remember that self-evaluation is worthless without honesty and objectivity.

Experienced teachers and administrators are usually happy to assist new teachers by observing classes and commenting on technique and procedures used. When peer evaluation is voluntarily requested, the teacher being evaluated is under less stress and is less hesitant to discuss shortcomings. The Lesson Observation Rating Form that is found in the appendix provides a format that is based on the four-step instructional process and is easily adaptable to most teaching situations. Try using it yourself by visiting other teachers, with their permission, and observing their teaching. Share your observations with them if they ask. Then have them reciprocate.

A comprehensive program of evaluation is an important part of every teaching-learning situation. Evaluation highlights the successes of the instructional process and its shortcomings. Ultimately, evaluation is used to improve the process.

Any evaluation must compare all elements of instruction and student learning with the objectives of the program or course. Techniques and devices must be developed to measure how well objectives are being met. Tests are used to determine student achievement, and several types of instruments are used to determine teacher effectiveness.

Students are capable of evaluating large portions of instruction. Teachers can do much to improve their instruction through honest self-appraisal, and peers and supervisors can observe classes and offer comments and helpful criticism.

It is important that all forms of evaluation be reliable and valid. The scope of this chapter prohibited a detailed discussion of these concepts, but the books and articles listed in the references section can provide you with assistance in the development, administration, and scoring of tests and evaluation instruments. The bibliography also contains chapters or sections that will help in determining test item effectiveness.

For Further Reading

Evaluation of Student Performance

Airasion, P.W., and Madaus, G.F. (1972). "Criterion-referenced Testing in the Classroom." *Measurement in Education* 3(4):1-8.

Archbald, D., and Newmann, F. (1988). *Beyond Standardized Testing: Authentic Academic Achievement in the Secondary School.* Reston, VA: NASSP Publications.

Bott, P.A. (1996). *Testing and Assessment in Occupational and Technical Education.* Needham Heights, MA: Allyn & Bacon.

DeGeorge, G.P. (1988). *Assessment and Placement of Language Minority Students: Procedures for Mainstreaming.* Silver Spring, MD: National Clearinghouse for Bilingual Education.

Diederich, P. (1960). *Shortcut Statistics for Teacher-Made Tests.* Princeton, NJ.: Educational Testing Service.

Erickson, R.C., and Wentling, T.L. (1976). *Measuring Student Growth: Techniques and Procedures for Occupational Education.* Boston: Allyn & Bacon.

Gronlund, N.E. (1981). *Measurement and Evaluation in Teaching.* New York: Macmillan.

Gronlund, N.E. (1968). *Constructing Achievement Tests.* Englewood Cliffs, N.J.: Prentice-Hall.

Hymes, D., Chafin, A., and Gonder, P. (1991). *The Changing Face of Testing and Assessment: Problems and Solutions.* Arlington, VA: American Association of School Administrators.

Mager, R.F. (1973). *Measuring Instructional Intent.* Belmont, CA: Fearon Publishers.

Miller, P. W., and Erickson, H.E. (1985). *Teacher-Written Student Tests: A Guide for Planning, Creating, Administering, and Assessing.* Washington, DC: National Education Association.

Mitchell, R. (1992). *Testing for Learning: How New Approaches to Evaluation Can Improve American Schools.* New York: The Free Press.

O'Neil, J. (1992, May). "Putting Performance Assessment to the Test." *Educational Leadership* 49(8):14–19.

Tyler, R.W. (1973). "Assessing Educational Achievement in the Affective Domain." Special report by the National Council on Measurement in Education, Vol. 4, No. 3, Spring.

Evaluation of Instruction

Airasian, P.W. (1993, October). "Teacher Assessment: Some Issues for Principals." *NAASP Bulletin* 77:55–65.

Gronlund, N.E. (1981). *Measurement and Evaluation in Teaching.* New York: Macmillan.

McNeil, J.D. (1973). *Toward Accountable Teachers: Their Appraisal and Improvement.* New York: Holt, Rinehart and Winston.

Popham, W.J. (1973). *Evaluating Instruction.* Englewood Cliffs, NJ: Prentice-Hall.

Smith, P.L. (1979). "The Generalizability of Student Ratings of Courses: Asking the Right Questions." *Journal of Educational Measurement* 16:77–88.

Terry, D.R., Thompson, R.L., and Evans, R.N. (1971). *Competencies for Teachers: Vocational Education Shows the Way.* Urbana, IL: University of Illinois.

Discussion Questions

1. What are the advantages and disadvantages of using objective tests?

   _____

   _____

   _____

2. List three advantages of (at least temporarily) returning test questions and answer sheets to students?

   _____

   _____

   _____

3. Why is it so difficult to accurately and reliably measure a person's attitude?

   _____

   _____

   _____

4. Is grading the same as evaluation? Why?

   _____

   _____

   _____

5. What are the major differences between administering performance tests and assessing student achievement with paper and pencil tests?

   _____

   _____

   _____

6. What should you do when you give an examination and the majority or all of the students do poorly? What are the things that you need to explore?

   _____

   _____

   _____

7. What rules, or principles of learning, are being practiced when we evaluate student achievement?

   _____

   _____

   _____

8. Who should participate in the process of evaluating instruction? Why? Describe their roles.

_____

_____

_____

9. Should the results of evaluation of instruction be used to determine whether teachers are retained on the job?

_____

_____

_____

Exercises

1. Twenty activities that teachers want students to be able to do upon completion of a course or unit of instruction are described below. The twenty activities are preceded by three descriptions of instructional levels. In the space that _precedes_ each activity, place the number that best describes the level of learning that would be required to achieve the knowledge or skill that is described. In the space _following_ each activity, indicate what type of test (objective, performance, essay) could be used to best indicate whether the student possesses the skill or knowledge. The first question is answered.

Levels of Learning

1. Requires remembering of facts and having the ability to follow directions; there are no manipulative skills required or learned.
2. Requires ability to recall facts and to interpret and translate diagrams, drawings, etc.; manipulative skills are sufficient to perform basic operations with supervision.
3. Requires application of principles, concepts, and theories to new problems and situations; manipulative skills are highly developed to the point that performance is sufficiently and smoothly executed.

__2__ Identify the various grades of lamb and mutton.   __objective__

_____ Set up and assist with periodontic treatments.   _____

_____ Compare operational principles of AC and DC motors.   _____

_____ Inspect and adjust passenger car brakes.   _____

_____ Trace the human circulatory system.   _____

_____ Classify six sets of fingerprints.   _____

_____   Weld with oxyacetylene equipment.   _____

_____   Read patterns on an oscilloscope.   _____

_____   Test hair for porosity.   _____

_____   Describe the effects of X-radiation.   _____

_____   Prepare paste-up for graphic reproduction.   _____

_____   Preserve physical evidence from a crime scene.   _____

_____   Identify the lymph-vascular system.   _____

_____   Proofread composed type.   _____

_____   Weld stainless steel to military specifications.   _____

_____ Trace the cooling system of a (vee) six-cylinder liquid-cooled engine.   _____

_____   Prepare and serve a chocolate souffle.   _____

_____   Install a moisture indicator.   _____

_____   Read a thermometer.   _____

_____   Identify insect damage to plants.   _____

2. Following the format described in this chapter and illustrated in the appendix, and using the objectives of the course that you teach or are preparing to teach, prepare a set of objective test questions of the following types. Indicate the correct answer for each item. Prepare a set of instructions to the student for completing each type of item.

    a. True-False (5 items)
    b. Multiple-Choice (5 items)
    c. Simple Completion (5 items)
    d. Short Answer Essay (2 items)
    e. Matching (at least 8 and 11 items, respectively, in the two columns)

3. Construct a performance examination to assess three of the psychomotor performance objectives for your course or program. Include a checklist for use in observing the examination. The checklist should have a rating scale that indicates the degree to which the specific performance is attained.

    For example, this examination might be to assess a student's performance on administering CPR, typing a manuscript, adjusting brakes, or taking a dental impression. The checklist is for your use in checking the student's performance (the steps in the process), and the rating scale is for assessing how well the task is performed. See the appendix for an example of a performance examination.

4. Using the information and data from this chapter and the appendix, develop an instrument that you can administer in your class to obtain feedback from your students as to how well you are doing as a teacher. Emphasize teaching style or technique, materials used, tests, and so on, but include the *human* aspects of caring, listening, and understanding.

Develop a scale that will allow for easy scoring of the instrument and explain on the form what the scale means. See the example in the appendix. If you are teaching, use the instrument once or twice in your class and tabulate and report the results.

Appendixes

Student Leadership Development Organizations

Completed Instructor's Lesson Plan

Textbook Evaluation Form

Checklist for Analyzing an Instructor's Lesson Plan

Code of Ethics

Community Resource Speakers Form

Audiovisual Resources Form

Sample Examination

Performance Test

Performance Test Rating Sheet

Lesson Observation Rating Form

Student Appraisal of Instruction

Student Leadership Development Organizations

- Business Professionals of America (office education)
  1701 N. Congress Ave.
  Austin, Texas 78701
  (800) 810-4603
  (512) 463-9692
- DECA, Distributive Education Clubs of America (marketing education)
  1908 Association Dr.
  Reston, VA 22091
  (703) 860-5000
- FBLA/Phi Beta Lambda, Future Business Leader of America (business leadership)
  1912 Association Dr.
  Reston, Virginia 22091
  (703) 860-3334
  FAX: (703)758-0749
- National FFA Organization, Future Farmers of America (agriculture)
  5632 Mount Vernon Memorial Hwy.
  P. O. Box 15160
  Alexandria, VA 22309-0160
  (703) 360-3600
  FAX: (703) 360-5524
- Future Homemakers of America/HERO (consumer and home economics)
  1910 Association Dr.
  Reston, VA 22091
  (703) 476-4900
- Health Occupations Students of America (health care)
  6309 N. O'Connor Rd., Ste. 215
  Irving, Texas 75039-3510
  (214) 506-9780
- National Postsecondary Agricultural Student Organization
  P. O. Box 15440
  Alexandria, VA 22309
  (703) 780-4922
- National Young Farmers Education Association (adult students in agriculture)
  P. O. Box 20326
  Montgomery, AL 36120-0326
  (334) 228-0097
- TSA, Technology Student Association (high-skill technology)
  1914 Association Dr.
  Reston, VA 22091
  (703) 860-9000
  FAX: (703) 758-4852
- VICA, Vocational Industrial Clubs of America (skill training and leadership)
  P. O. Box 456
  Onalaska, Wis. 54650
  (800) 321-8422

INSTRUCTOR'S LESSON PLAN

SUBJECT: Medication Administration	**INSTRUCTOR:** Ima Nurse

TITLE OF LESSON: Intramuscular Medication Administration

TIME PERIOD (TOTAL): 30 minutes

TYPE OF LESSON: Lecture

PLACE: Classroom

TRAINING AIDS: Handouts (diagrams)

OBJECTIVE(S): See syllabus and Introduction notes

INSTRUCTOR REFERENCES: Text books, Introduction to patient care, and Pharmacologic Basis of Patient Care

STUDENT REFERENCES AND HOMEWORK: Student notes, handouts, review task analysis for return demonstration (second lesson).

TIME	LESSON OUTLINE	KEY POINTS AND AID CUES

00:00	<u>Introduction</u>
	
	Good morning. The topic of today's lesson is intramuscular medication administration, or giving shots.
	
	Today, you will learn important information that will assist you in performing intramuscular injections with knowledge, safety, and with confidence. Giving injections is a skill that you will perform over and over in your career as a nurse, so it is important that you feel secure in your knowledge and skill in performing injections.
	
	Upon completion of this and the next two lessons, you will be able to perform intramuscular injections in a number of different sites on the body. You will practice and perfect this procedure using fruit and your classmates.
	
	As previously learned there are several common routes for administration of medications.
	    Oral- Nasal- Ophthalmic- Inhalation-
	    Sublingual- Rectal- Parenteral- NG
	
	Today our focus will be on IM's only.
	*Remember that a different approach should be taken when administering injections. Even the strongest, and most self-sufficient man can become a "terrified youngster" when approached with a needle or syringe.
		
		Handout, teacher notes
		
		Review
		
		Personal story, classmate Pam - first time giving an injection

TIME	LESSON OUTLINE	KEY POINTS AND AID CUES
	<u>Development</u>	
00:03	1.0 Define intramuscular	Teacher notes, Handout on layers of tissue, Define <u>vascularity</u>
00:05	2.0 Review Advantages/Disadvantages of IM injections.	
	3.0 Sites of Intramuscular Injections 3.1 Deltoid 3.2 Ventrogluteal 3.3 Dorsal Gluteal 3.4 Lateral thigh	Handout, teacher notes
00:10	4.0 Important Information before administering medications 4.1 Proper identification of Dr. order 4.2 Classification of medications 4.3 Adverse reactions/allergic reactions 4.4 Special nursing actions needed before administering medication 4.5 Appropriate safety measures 4.6 Appropriate documentation of medication	Put on Chalkboard Ask students for examples Use O/H
00:15	5.0 Five "Rights" of medication administration 5.1 Right medication 5.2 Right patient 5.3 Right dosage 5.4 Right time 5.5 Right route	 Use O/H
00:20	6.0 Equipment needed 6.1 Syringe, appropriate size 6.2 Needle, appropriate size 6.3 Medication 6.4 Alcohol swab 6.5 Adhesive bandage	Have available equipment for students to see
00:22	7.0 Four factors to consider when choosing injection site 7.1 Anatomically safe 7.2 Free of bruises or sore areas 7.3 Free of hardened skin (scars) 7.4 Free of abrasions	
00:28	<u>Application</u> Review important points through discussion and questions (summary) In the next lesson, a lecture with demonstration, you will participate in a return demo. of drawing up medication, preparing site, and performing an IM injection (using an orange).	Review, ask questions
00:29	<u>Evaluation</u> Evaluated by students' response to discussion and questions.	

Textbook Evaluation Form

Title of Book   _____

Author's Name   _____

Date of Publishing   _____

Number of Pages   _____

Price to Students $_____

Use a scale of 0 to 5, with 0 representing nonexistent or inadequate, and 5 representing excellent. Rate textbooks for their potential in your program.

Physical Features

1. The binding is durable and the book is of convenient size 0   1   2   3   4   5
2. Quality of paper and printing is appropriate 0   1   2   3   4   5
3. Tables, diagrams, and pictures are accurate, effective, and up-to-date... 0   1   2   3   4   5

Organization

4. Entire units of instruction.. 0   1   2   3   4   5
5. Index is thorough.. 0   1   2   3   4   5
6. Table of contents is accurate and detailed........................... 0   1   2   3   4   5
7. Content is presented in a logical order 0   1   2   3   4   5

Content

8. Material included is sufficient to make the book valuable and useful.. 0   1   2   3   4   5
9. Subject matter is up-to-date.. 0   1   2   3   4   5
10. Available research material has been used............................ 0   1   2   3   4   5
11. Provision is made for student review and summary 0   1   2   3   4   5

Style and Vocabulary

12. The book is written in an interesting and understandable style 0   1   2   3   4   5
13. The reading level is appropriate 0   1   2   3   4   5
14. Suggestions for evaluation and student activities are meaningful and stimulating.. 0   1   2   3   4   5

Author's Background

Checklist for Analyzing an Instructor's Lesson Plan

1. In the HEADING have you included:
   a. Title, total time of lesson, and place?
   b. List of training aids, including tools and equipment needed?
   c. References?
   d. Statement of the student performance objective(s)?
   e. Other information dictated by need or by personal desires?

2. Does the INTRODUCTION:
   a. Tie this lesson in with previous lesson(s) or with the students' life experiences?
   b. Provide for review where desirable?
   c. Show the value of learning this material?
   d. Serve as an interest-arousing factor?
   e. Firmly establish the objectives of the lesson and the resultant student performance?

3. Does the DEVELOPMENT provide:
   a. An outline of new material arranged in suitable form?
   b. Development from known to unknown and from simple to complex?
   c. For the training of the students?
   d. Complete outlines for demonstrations, if any?
   e. Examples, illustrations, and devices for clarifying material?
   f. Integration, where possible, with other training?
   g. Directions for the use of aids?
   h. Sketches for chalkboard work (if the board is to be used)?
   i. Key questions and desired answers?
   j. A chronology of time (left column)?

4. Does the SUMMARY:
   a. Review important points and state conclusions reached?
   b. Tie-in with lessons to follow?

5. Is the ENTIRE PLAN:
   a. Screened so that all material points toward the objective(s)?
   b. Provided with smooth and purposeful transitions?
   c. In a form that makes it usable during a class period?
   d. Practical with regard to time-material relationships?

Code of Ethics of the Teaching Profession

State of California

PREAMBLE

The educator believes in the worth and dignity of human beings. The educator recognizes the supreme importance of the pursuit of truth, devotion to excellence, and the nurture of democratic citizenship. The educator regards as essential to these goals the protection of freedom to learn and to teach and the guarantee of equal educational opportunity for all. The educator accepts the responsibility to practice the profession according to the highest ethical standards.

The educator recognizes the magnitude of the responsibility being accepted in choosing a career in education and engages individually and collectively with other educators to judge colleagues, and to be judged by them, in accordance with the provisions of this code.

PRINCIPLE I

Commitment to the Student. The educator measures success by the progress of each student toward realization of potential as a worthy and effective citizen. The educator therefore works to stimulate the spirit of inquiry, the acquisition of knowledge and understanding, and the thoughtful formulation of worthy goals. In fulfilling these goals, the educator:

(a) Encourages the student to independent action in the pursuit of learning and provides access to varying points of view.

(b) Prepares the subject carefully, presents it to the students without distortion and—within the limits of time and curriculum—gives all points of view a fair hearing.

(c) Protects the health and safety of students.

(d) Honors the integrity of students and influences them through constructive criticism rather than by ridicule and harassment.

(e) Provides for participation in educational programs without regard to race, color, creed, national origin or sex—both in what is taught and how it is taught.

(f) Neither solicits nor involves them or their parents in schemes for commercial gain thereby insuring that professional relationships with students shall not be used for private advantage.

(g) Shall keep in confidence information that has been obtained in the course of professional service, unless disclosure serves professional purposes or is required by law.

PRINCIPLE II

Commitment to the Public. The educator believes that democratic citizenship in its highest form requires dedication to the principles of our democratic heritage. The educator shares with all other citizens the responsibility for the development of sound public policy and assumes full political and citizenship responsibilities. The educator bears particular responsibility for the development of policy relating to the extension of educational opportunities for all and for interpretation of educational programs and policies to the public. In fulfilling these goals, the educator:

(a) Has an obligation to support the profession and institution and not to misrepresent them in public discussion. When being critical in public, the educator has an obligation not to distort the facts. When speaking or writing about policies, the educator must take adequate precautions to distinguish the educator's private views from the official position of the institution.

(b) Does not interfere with a colleague's exercise of political and citizenship rights and responsibilities.

(c) Ensures that institutional privileges shall not be used for private gain. Does not exploit pupils, their parents, colleagues, nor the school system itself for private advantage. Does not accept gifts or favors that might impair or appear to impair professional judgment nor offer any favor, service, or thing of value to obtain special advantage.

PRINCIPLE III

Commitment to the Profession. The educator believes that the quality of the services of the education profession directly influences the Nation and its citizens. The educator therefore exerts every effort to raise professional standards, to improve service, to promote a climate in which the exercise of professional judgment is encouraged, and to achieve conditions which attract persons worthy of trust to careers in education. In fulfilling these goals, the educator:

(a) Accords just and equitable treatment to all members of the profession in the exercise of their professional rights and responsibilities.

(b) Does not use coercive means or promise special treatment in order to influence professional decisions of colleagues.

(c) Does not misrepresent personal professional qualifications.

(d) Does not misrepresent the professional qualifications of colleagues, and will discuss these qualifications fairly and accurately when discussion serves professional purposes.

(e) Applies for, accepts, offers, and assigns positions or responsibility on the basis of professional preparation and legal qualifications.

(f) Uses honest and effective methods of administering educational responsibility. Conducts professional business through proper channels. Does not assign unauthorized persons to educational tasks. Uses time granted for its intended purposes. Does not misrepresent conditions of employment. Lives up to the letter and spirit of contracts.

UNPROFESSIONAL CONDUCT

This code is a set of ideals which the teaching profession expects its members to honor and follow. Any violation is unprofessional. However, to constitute unprofessional conduct and cause for suspension, revocation or denial of a certification document, or renewal thereof, such violations shall be only those which either involve jeopardy to student welfare; evidence malice, serious incompetency or bad judgment; or show a consistent pattern of misconduct.

This code of ethics is not an exhaustive enumeration of acts or conduct which constitute unprofessional conduct.

PROVISIONS NOT APPLICABLE TO COMMUNITY COLLEGE TEACHERS

The provisions of this article do not apply to any person while serving in grades thirteen or fourteen or in any course taught under the jurisdiction of a community college. Such person, however, may be subject to disciplinary action for unprofessional conduct when the person or agency having responsibility therefor independently determines such person has committed an act or acts involving unprofessional conduct irrespective of whether such act or acts are or are not prohibited by this article.

California Administrative Code - Title 5 Regulations
Sections 80130-80132 - Adopted 5/20/77

EXECUTIVE SECRETARY, COMMISSION FOR
TEACHER PREPARATION AND LICENSING

CHAIRMAN, COMMISSION FOR TEACHER
PREPARATION AND LICENSING

Community Resource Speakers Form

NAME	POSITION	BUSINESS ADDRESS	TELEPHONE	TOPIC/AREA OF INTEREST

Audiovisual Resources Form

MEDIUM	TITLE	LOCATION	COST	FOR UNIT	RATING

Sample Examination

Name _____ Date _____

General Instructions

This examination consists of a number of true-false, multiple-choice, matching, and completion items. Instructions are provided for answering each type of question. A separate sheet is provided for your answers. DO NOT make any marks on the examination itself. The total examination is worth 50 points and 10 percent of your final grade.

True-False Instructions

A number of statements are listed below; some are true and some are false. If any part of a statement is false, the entire statement is false. Make your decision with regard to each statement and make an X through the appropriate letter on your answer sheet. Each true-false item is worth one point.

1. A good rule to follow in test construction is to have the first question a difficult one.
2. If you wanted students to learn how to operate an eight-inch radial arm saw, the most appropriate teaching method would include demonstration, practice, and drill.
3. Determining grades based solely on test results is the safest and most fair way.
4. The best method of measuring cognitive gain is to use a performance test.
5. Test items should range from *relatively easy* to *difficult,* with the majority falling in the middle range.

Multiple-Choice Instructions

Each of the incomplete statements or questions listed below is followed by several possible answers. From these, select the best answer for each test item, and then, on the Scantron sheet that is provided, darken the letter of that response. Each item is worth two points.

6. True-false items are most useful for measuring learning in the
   a. cognitive domain.
   b. affective domain.
   c. psychomotor domain.
   d. all domains.

7. A performance objective containing the phrase "will demonstrate their responsibility" is most likely seeking behavior in the _____ domain.
   a. cognitive
   b. affective
   c. psychomotor
   d. general

8. Learning depends upon the learner's
   a. intelligence more than any other variable.
   b. skill in performing motor tasks.
   c. perceptual capacity only.
   d. having motives satisfied to some degree.

9. What is the first step in learning?
   a. when a new impression is recalled
   b. the preparation step
   c. the presentation step
   d. recognizing the need to learn

10. The most common approach to grading is in the form of
    a. written reports.
    b. conferences.
    c. narrative reports.
    d. numbers.
    e. letters, such as A-F.

Matching Instructions

In the following group of questions, column A consists of words or terms. Match those words or terms in column A with the words or phrase in column B that are most closely related to or define them. Column B items may be used only once. Put the letter of the correct response in the appropriate place on your answer sheet. Each item is worth one point.

A	*B*
11. Cam	A. Collects exhaust gases from exhaust valves or ports.
12. Carburetor	B. Admits fuel mixture directly to the cylinder.
13. Crankcase	C. Regulates the opening and closing of the intake valve.
14. Cylinder	D. Ignites air and fuel mixture.
15. Exhaust Manifold	E. Effects a gas tight seal between piston and cylinder.
(at least 5)	(add at least 3 more than in A)

Completion Instructions

A blank space is found in each of the following incomplete statements. Write the word in the appropriate space on your answer sheet that will make each statement complete and true. Each item is worth two points.

16. Tests that measure knowledge of facts and figures deal with the _____ domain.

17. A good rule for completion items is to omit only one _____ .

18. The best test for measuring how well a student can actually perform a specific skill would be a _____ test.

19. When using completion questions, there is little chance for a student to _____ the correct answer.

20. The arithmetical average of all scores on a test is called the _____ .

PERFORMANCE TEST
MACHINING AN ALUMINUM SQUARE BLOCK

NAME: _____   DATE: _____

MATERIAL NEEDED

All materials and tools will be provided.

1- Material: $2 \times 2 \times 2$ inch aluminum square block 6061—T6.
2- ½" dia. × 6.00 long steel rod.
3- 2.50 dia. fly cutter.
4- Bridgeport vertical milling machine—series II.
5- 1–2" outside micrometer.
6- 6" machinist combination square set.
7- .001 increment dial indicator.
8- 6" vise.
9- Soft hammer.
10- ½" parallel set.
11- Medium flat file.

STUDENT INSTRUCTIONS

- This performance test is designed to measure your machine skills as your work in machining an aluminum square block.
- Using the materials and tools furnished, you will machine an aluminum block to the dimensions show on the drawing below.

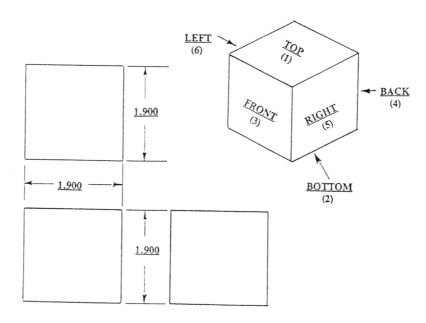

PROCEDURES

- Using the Bridgeport vertical milling machine and the dimensions shows:
  A- Break all burrs and sharp edges of the 2.00" square block with the medium flat file.
  B- Locate, secure and indicate vise on machine's table.
  C- Locate top surface (#1) against fixed visejaw, tighten vise with ½" rod against movable visejaw, tap part down with soft hammer, machine front surface (#3) of block to a 100% cleanup with 2.50 dia. fly cutter.
  D- Remove block from vise, rotate so that the machined side is against fixed visejaw, machine the bottom surface (#2) to a 100% cleanup.
  E- Remove block from vise, rotate again, insert ½" parallel set underneath the block and machine the back surface (#4) to finish dimension 1.900.
  F- Machine top surface (#1) finish to 1.900 dimension.
  G- Set up block with back surface (#4) located against the machinist square, machine right surface (#5) to a 100% cleanup.
  H- Reverse part and machine left surface (#6) finish to 1.900 dimension.
  I- Deburr and break all sharp edges with file.

LIST OF SKILLS TO BE VALUED

1- Use of medium flat file to deburr sharp edges.
2- Use of indicator.
3- Use of 1–2" outside micrometer.
4- Use of machinist square.
5- Use of soft hammer.
6- Use of ½" dia. steel rod, ½" parallel set and visejaws.
7- Loading and unloading tool on milling machine.
8- Calculating proper speed and feed.
9- Set up procedures, following instructions, and machining techniques.

STANDARDS

A- Tolerance for all dimensions are plus and minus .002 of an inch.
B- Indicated visejaws to within .001 of an inch (straightness and flatness).
C- Calculate and set machine's speed and feed to correct RPM and IPM.
D- All machined surface finished to be within 125 microinches.
E- Deburr all sharp edges to within .015/.025, using the medium flat file.
F- Inspect all dimensions with 1–2" micrometer.
G- Students must achieve a minimum of 70 percent of the points in each category to pass. Failure of one category constitutes failure of the entire examination.

PERFORMANCE TEST RATING SHEET

STUDENT'S NAME _____   **DATE** _____

RATED BY _____   **SCORE** _____

RATING SCALE — MACHINING A BLOCK

SKILLS	POINTS POSSIBLE	GIVEN
1. Uses medium flat file, deburrs sharp edges to within .015/.025.	10	
2. Uses indicator to indicate visejaws to within .001 of an inch (straightness and flatness).	10	
3. Uses 1–2" outside micrometer to measure all dimensions to within + and – .002.	10	
4. Uses machinist square to set up block perpendicular in visejaws.	5	
5. Uses soft hammer to tap part down for flatness.	5	
6. Uses 1/2" diameter rod, 1/2" parallel set, and visejaws to locate and secure part for proper maching operations.	15	
7. Applies proper techniques to load and unload tool safely.	5	
8. Calculate correct speed and feed for aluminum 6061–T6 material.	10	
9. Follow set-up procedures and instructions, check part for flatness, squareness and machined finish (125 microinches max.). Check all dimensions to within specifications. Is the part free of burrs and sharp edges?	30	
TOTAL POINTS	**100**	

LESSON OBSERVATION RATING FORM

Name of Person Giving Lesson _____

Location _____

Date _____   Time _____

Class Level (Grade) _____

Number of Students _____

Title of the Lesson _____

Instructions

The purpose of this rating scale, which is based on the four-step instructional system, is to create a consciousness on your part of the vital points that seriously affect the success of a teacher. Ratings are of value only if they are made with complete frankness. You may wish to clarify some of the ratings by making comments in the space provided. A rating of "4" would be very good, or high, while a rating of "1" would be poor.

Motivation

(Step 1) Time spent _____ minutes.

	4	3	2	1	N/A
1. How well did the teacher "prepare" the class?					
2. Did the teacher find out what the students knew about the lesson?					

Presentation

(Step 2) Time spent _____ minutes.

	4	3	2	1	N/A
3. Were trade terms and technical words explained?					
4. How well was the lesson held to the topic?					
5. Were practical examples used to clarify points in the lesson?					
6. Did the teacher refrain from "talking to the board"?					
7. Was the chalkboard work clear?					
8. Did the teacher look at ALL students?					
9. Were the visual aids used effectively?					
10. Was the lesson summarized?					
11. Overall quality of the demonstration, experiment, or lecture was					

Application

(Step 3) Time spent _____ minutes.

	4	3	2	1	N/A
12. Was the teacher successful in keeping the discussion related to the subject?					
13. Did the teacher maintain the interest of the class?					
14. Did the teacher stimulate student participation in the lesson?					
15. Was there a frequent check-up for understanding of the things taught?					
16. Were the questions clear?					
17. Were good questioning techniques used?					

Evaluation

(Step 4) Time spent _____ minutes.

	4	3	2	1	N/A
18. How well was the lesson summarized and student understanding checked?					
19. Quality of the testing?					

Personality Traits

20. Voice quality					
21. Enthusiasm					
22. Posture					
23. Mannerisms					
24. Use of English					
25. Appropriate Dress					
26. Professionalism					

Preparation by the Teacher

27. Did the lesson appear to be well-planned?					
28. Were all charts, tools, tests, films, instruction sheets, and other aids ready for use?					
29. Your overall rating of the lesson					

30. How would you characterize the mode of instruction used in this lesson? (If more than one applies, check all.)

_____ Lecture   _____ Multimedia oriented

_____ Demonstration   _____ Resource speaker

_____ Discussion   _____ Role-playing

_____ Small groups   _____ Other

_____ Supervised study

Comments:

STUDENT APPRAISAL OF INSTRUCTION

Date _____ Course _____

Teacher's Name _____

Think of all the other teachers that you have had and compare the instruction that you have received in this class with your ideal instructor. Draw a circle around the number that best represents your appraisal of the present instruction as compared with your ideal instructor. Use the following code when making your comparison.

5—Excellent : Unusually effective; very knowledgeable; definitely superior; very appropriate.

4—Good   : Effective; knowledgeable; above average; unusually superior.

3—Average : Usually effective; good command of the subject; OK.

2—Poor   : Ineffective; below average.

1—Very Poor : Detrimental in all respects; not on a par with others.

  1. Demonstrated knowledge of latest information in the field studied 5   4   3   2   1

  2. Relationship of assignments to course objectives 5   4   3   2   1

  3. Demonstrated ability to communicate facts, concepts, and ideas 5   4   3   2   1

  4. Demonstrated knowledge of course and program requirements 5   4   3   2   1

  5. Quality and relevance of reading materials 5   4   3   2   1

  6. Quality of student involvement during class. 5   4   3   2   1

  7. Appropriateness of assigned work load 5   4   3   2   1

  8. Completeness with which questions are answered 5   4   3   2   1

  9. Relationship of class presentations with course objectives 5   4   3   2   1

10. Demonstrated planning and organization of the class 5   4   3   2   1

11. Demonstrated ability to cause learning to occur 5   4   3   2   1

12. Use of appropriate media or instructional techniques 5   4   3   2   1

13. Challenging learning experience provided. 5   4   3   2   1

14. Use of fair and appropriate evaluation techniques. 5   4   3   2   1

Please feel free to make any comments you wish on the reverse.

Index